THE OPENING
OF THE
AMERICAN MIND
Social Problems—
Solutions
and Reforms

*To a worthy and
generous parishioner
with gratitude for
your donation
towards our
building fund*

C. Antonio Provost

THE OPENING OF THE AMERICAN MIND
Social Problems—Solutions and Reforms

C. Antonio Provost

First edition
Library of Congress Catalog No. 89-64102

Copyright © 1990 by C. Antonio Provost

Libra Publishers, Inc.
3089C Clairemont Drive, Suite 383
San Diego, California 92117

Manufactured in the United States of America

ISBN 0-87212-235-2

The paper used in this publication meets the minimum requirements of the American National Standard for Information Sciences—Permanence of Paper
for Printed Library Materials, ANSI Z39.48-1984.

ABOUT THE AUTHOR

C. Antonio Provost was born in Colon, Panama, in 1910. At the age of thirteen he came to Los Angeles, becoming a U.S. citizen in 1934. He served in the army in WWII for three and a half years in the Southwest Pacific theater, reaching the rank of staff sergeant.

Mr. Provost retired from the U.S. Postal Service after thirty years, and at age 65 continued his education at Saddleback College where he earned an A.A. degree. He then went on to acquire a degree in philosophy with a minor in sociology and a certificate in gerontology from California State University at Long Beach. He also took courses in theater arts and journalism at Mira Costa College in Oceanside.

His published books include: *The Birth of the Modern Renaissance* and *The Sexual Revolution: Its Impact on Society.* In addition, he coauthored *The Senior Olympics—With Findings Pertaining to Health and Longevity.*

His poems have appeared in the *American Collegiate Poets Anthology,* and he produced a televised, 15-minute video-docudrama based on his script: "The Plight of Philosophers: Socrates, Plato and Aristotle."

He continues to be active in community affairs and is involved in Senior Olympics programs, participating in such events as tennis, racquetball, swimming, and track and field. He has already won gold, silver, and bronze medals, and in the 1990 Senior Olympics in San Diego, he earned three medals.

And Mr. Provost still finds time to be active in a national fraternal religious-oriented church organization and to participate as program director and vice president of the Oceanside chapter of the National Association of Retired Federal Employees. He is also a volunteer worker for the Oceanside City Library. Little wonder he was selected as the most active senior citizen of the year at the Del Mar Fair in 1989.

Mr. Provost has been married for over 48 years and has a son, daughter, granddaughter, and grandson.

CONTENTS

Illustrations

ACKNOWLEDGMENTS

I am deeply grateful to Dr. Francisco L. Peccorini, one of my philosophy professors at California State University at Long Beach, for his teaching and inspiration. Upon his retirement, he gave his life for his country, El Salvador. A dual citizen of the United States and his native land, he was martyred by a communist faction.

I also owe him a debt of gratitude for his foreword to my book, *The Sexual Revolution: Its Impact on Society.*

I also owe a debt of gratitude to my wife, Irene, for her sacrifices in putting up with and without me during our almost 50 years of marriage. Without her forbearance and suggestions I could not have accomplished as much in the fields of literature, philosophy, and education.

I am most grateful for the preliminary editing of my manuscript and the very constructive criticism by Paul H. Hallett. He devoted much valuable time from his busy schedule and has encouraged me to continue to present valid solutions to some of our major social problems.

Many thanks to Dr. Threlkeld for his comments, observations, and kind words.

FOREWORD

In my brief acquaintance with Mr. Provost, through this book and a previous one, I see him as a man of great sincerity and high purpose. This book, admirably entitled *The Opening of the American Mind,* grasps the sore need for reeducation in America today in the fullness of its moral dimension—a side neglected by too many educators.

In modern educational philosophy, the general defense of those who reject the teaching of natural law morality in the public schools is that this touches on religion—and the teaching of religion is forbidden by the First Amendment.

Provost rightly answers that we have carried the separation [of church and state] concept too far. As he says: "We need the instrument of religion; we need pillars of morality." Teaching any view of life that is opposed to religion is itself teaching a kind of religion, and a bad one. The author brings this out very well.

In Chapter V he turns a searching eye on what I consider the worst folly of the modern educational system—the attempt to teach sexuality without any consideration of what it is meant to be by the law of nature. Educators generally are too much under the delusion that the violent sexual instinct can be headed off by preventive measures that go under the name of "safe sex" [in an amoral sex course].

Provost shows very well that the fanning of the flames of sexual desire by pornography, which reaches even to the television screen—and by miseducation in the schools—has resulted in a conflagration that can be checked only by moral restraints inculcated by sound education. He does not directly allude to what religion and the natural law ethic teach about the right use of sex, but he cites apt quotations from what philosophers like Plato and Aristotle have said about the need to control the sexual appetite. These lessons are rounded out and made specific by impressive quotations from certain modern social scientists and philosophers, as well as from well-balanced educators whose principles have been so lamentably ignored by much of the modern school system.

The author's use of the towering figure of Alexis Carrel in support of the control of the unruly sex instinct through sublimation and the conservation of sexual energy is aptly made, and the quotations he draws from this and other sources are in my opinion the most valuable in his book. On the other hand, he does not fear to rebuke even so great a name as that of Dr. Karl Menninger when he sanctions the abominable practice of masturbation.

Provost is enlightening in his explanations of biofeedback, a method by which sexual tension can be reduced by diverting the sex impulse into productive channels. This is not an effortless exercise—but no attempts at moral self-control without effort is possible. From the explanation we see here, it should be richly rewarding.

Mr. Provost is one of those rare souls who does not confound "thinking for yourself" with thinking arbitrarily or not thinking at all. The reader should benefit from his loyalty to tradition and common sense.

—Paul Hallett

(Mr. Hallett is a Catholic journalist and author of several non-fiction books; his latest is *Witness To Permanence,* Ignatius Press, San Francisco, 1987. He has been a regular contributor to the *National Catholic Register* and is one of the contributing editors.)

FOREWORD

Mr. Provost: I have received your thesis and can find no fault in the contents. I have spent over forty years taking care of people and their sexual problems plus their mistakes—infections, infidelity, unwanted pregnancies, and marital maladjustments. My successes and failures cannot be summarized here. I tried to do my best.

Your references to Socrates and the works of Plato and Aristotle pertaining to human sexual behavior could have been helped by including the teachings of Buddha, Confucius, and later Mohammed. These teachers also taught self-control and sublimation in a certain sense. Buddha taught that worldly life cannot give final happiness, and that one should not be completely self-indulgent and cannot be too strict with oneself.

Of all the creatures on this earth, only man has the exercise of free will. He can self-destruct or he can create unlimited works of art, music, science, etc. Yet, he is also endowed with the instincts and the passions of the so-called lower animals.

Arnold Toynbee, the British historian and author,

said: "Without our code of laws, imperfect as they are, there would be no civilization." We are facing the dilemma of legal abortion—the pressure groups are powerful and I pray we will be able to find a solution to this problem. Wars and conflicts occur when logic and practical solutions fail. We must keep on trying and perhaps utopia will be reached someday.

You have included some constructive measures for reforms, especially in the field of education.

L. Duncan Threlkeld, M.D., Emeritus Clinical Professor of Gynecology and Obstetrics, Oklahoma University Health Science Center and member of the Oklahoma State Medical Association Committee for Legislative Affairs

INTRODUCTION

At the moment, politicians with eyes glued to television and ears bent by pollsters are simply incapable of providing the leadership we need. It is the responsibility of intellectuals [of the right caliber] to raise their voices, and the responsibility of citizens to listen to what they say.

Mark C. Taylor, Director of the Center for the Humanities and Social Sciences at Williams College. (From the Los Angeles Times April 15, 1990 Book Review Section.)

Since no one can deny that we are in need of social reforms and that the present trend of criminal activities and unethical behavior—from the white collar workers and some of our political leaders to the lowest elements in our beleaguered society—it appears certain that efforts must be made by all concerned citizens to rally to the cause. We must do our utmost in order to institute remedial measures for stemming the tide of criminality and widespread unethical behavior.

The magnitude of our complex major social problems appears to be almost overwhelming, but we cannot afford to allow the difficulties in reaching our ultimate goals to deter us. Real and lasting solutions can be found.

It is quite evident that no viable solutions have been devised, no genuine formula to end our social retrogression for curbing the incidence of crime. In order to effectively alleviate this situation which has been devastating to many people, a better kind of education is necessary.

There are root causes for our social problems, and although there are no easy solutions, through concentrated study and analysis of the works of philosophers and sociologists—and the application of some creative thinking—answers can be found.

Philosophy is indeed a most potent tool for bringing about constructive social as well as political changes which can save our country. By turning to the "Great Books," by studying what the greatest of all philosophers have written and concluded, we can begin to go forward.

We must also look to contemporary writers who also are deeply concerned about the present trend toward social disintegration and chaos. I am deeply indebted to them for their contributions.

I also give credit to some of the sermons I have heard and my reading of many epistles and gospels which many people ignore and often ridicule.

I am also grateful to Professor Peter L. Berger for his book, *Invitation to Sociology: A Humanistic Perspective,* and his revelations concerning the defects in the field of sociology.

THE OPENING OF THE AMERICAN MIND
Social Problems—Solutions and Reforms

Chapter I

SOCIOLOGICAL FINDINGS AND IMPLICATIONS

What exactly is sociology? It is generally and in the broadest sense defined as: "The science which investigates the laws that regulate human society in all its grades; the science which treats the general structure of society, the laws of its development, and the progress of civilization." To be more explicit, we might add that it also deals with the causes and effects of human behavior on society as well as on the individual. Thus, sociology embraces vast areas of human activity and therefore offers a field for never-ending research.

We who are senior citizens may not live to see much of the changes we are attempting to make in society, but if we lay the foundation, if we strive to bring about the urgently needed reforms in education, the younger generation and those to follow will be most grateful for what we have done to bring about a far more humane and civilized society.

1

The older generation has witnessed and read about the disastrous social retrogression, and with their perspective, they can see what has to be done to *make a difference for the common good.*

Those without this perspective may sincerely believe that all's well and that no changes are necessary. But without doubt there are many who will welcome new ideas and ways of coping with today's problems.

What are some of these problems? Why am I and so many of our citizens and noncitizens so concerned about them? Let us study some of the statistics: The F.B.I. over a period of approximately 30 years, has provided evidence which shows that crime in the U.S. has risen steadily, and there is no sign that it will decrease. The 1967 World Almanac and Book of Facts records the following F.B.I. statistics: From 1960 through 1965 the number of serious crimes increased by 46% although the population increased by only 6%. The crimes against property rose by 47%. The 1977 edition showed a 10% increase over 1974; of all crimes reported, the percentage was up from 1% to 14%. The 1981 edition showed violent crimes up 4.4%. The 1989 edition showed that from 1986 through 1987 there was an increase in the crime index total from 2.5% to 20.5%. Percentage per 100,000 inhabitants increased from plus 1.4 to plus 8.1. Such statistics clearly indicate we are losing ground in our attempt to reduce the rate of crime. If all crimes were reported, of course, the statistics would be even more alarming. It is estimated and acknowledged that only a fraction of rape cases are reported, and very few of domestic violence and sexual abuse. What does this portend? The signs are very clear; other reports are equally disturbing.

Some researchers, journalists, and authors fully understand the nature of our social problems. Many of them have reported their findings:

Juvenile sex offenders and their crimes are not the sort of topic that our society likes to think about, and that's a part of the problem. But reluctance to discuss these tragic youngsters and their offenses can no longer mask a growing crisis: America is awash in reported and unreported sexual crimes committed by juvenile offenders. The nation was shocked into awareness about the problem recently by the case of the woman jogger who was assaulted and raped by a gang of juveniles. But rapes by juveniles (mostly against other juveniles) are becoming distressingly commonplace. The National Center for Juvenile Justice reports that between 1976 and 1986, the national arrest rate for 13- and 14-year-olds accused of rape doubled to 40 arrests per 100,000 children. The arrest rate for lesser sexual crimes in that age category increased by 80% over the last decade. Perhaps most tragically of all, experts say the age at which juveniles become sexual offenders drops with each passing year. Many of these juvenile offenders have themselves been victims of sexual abuse as children.[1]

An author criticizing Dr. Alfred Kinsey's works and remarks pertaining to sexual child abuse stated:

Another bombshell disguised as social science "research" whose ravages are still visible today, was released in the

3

1940s with the aid of tax-free money. It was the two-volume Kinsey Report, which became a runaway best seller and was widely quoted in social, academic circles of the day. . . . Among other things, the Kinsey Report condoned homosexuality, pre-marital sex for women and even child-molesting, because, said Kinsey, "the molester of children may have contributed favorably to their later sexual development."[2]

These reports indicate the gravity of the problem and what must be done in order to bring about genuine reform in this vital area. Other authors who have studied this social problem have voiced their views pertaining to this most controversial issue which will be discussed in detail in Chapter V.

An extreme permissiveness of an almost pathological nature has engulfed a considerable part of the American population, not unlike a fast-growing cancer. Applauded, promoted, fully approved by the liberal intellects, the permissible movement was declared by them as a social revolution, as the beginning of a New America. Permissiveness contaminated all sides of American life. . . . Uncontrolled freedom of sex reached national proportions, with a growing and dangerous epidemic of venereal diseases. . . . I decided to write this book, telling how a biologist sees the causes of the extreme permissiveness which affects our society and what physiological and biological factors are involved in it. . . . It is in the field of sexuality that the influence of the permissiveness syndrome has reached its height . . . and in America: The liberals are leading the campaign for freedom of sex. . . .[3]

4

It should be quite apparent why we are having social problems which stem from the "sexual freedom" movement. Although such admonitions appeared in various publications in 1971 and several years later, instead of heeding the judicious suggestions of these authors, the situation grew increasingly worse. There is far more "sexual freedom" and unethical human sexual behavior than ever. Dr. Sokoloff's revealing "Sex in America"[4] exposes the nature of the problem.

A famous sociologist indicated how important it is to include philosophy in dealing with sociological problems. Professor Peter L. Berger of Rutgers' sociology department wrote:

> Openness to the humanistic scope of sociology further implies an ongoing communication with other disciplines that are vitally concerned with exploring the human condition. The most important of these are history and philosophy. The foolishness of some sociological work, especially in this country, could be easily avoided by a measure of literacy in these two areas. . . . As to philosophical literacy, it would not only prevent the methodological naivete [the quality or state of being naive in their work] of some sociologists, but would also be conducive to a more adequate grasp of the phenomena themselves that the sociologist wishes to investigate.[5]

Indeed sociologists who skillfully employ genuine philosophy in their explorations into the phenomena, will be in a far better position to arrive at valid solutions to the complex problems that affect society.

Any sociologist who fails to realize the value of philosophy to understanding the problems is not worthy of the name. The study of philosophy which pertains to human behavior in all its forms, especially ethical doctrines covering human sexual behavior, is an absolute necessity.

The sociologist who utilizes philosophy can provide a very simple and therefore all the more useful insight to men trying to find their way through the jungle of competing world views [and the conflicting philosophies which are tantamount to a destructive way of life and the ruination of society].[6]

Other authors have delved into the field of sociology. They reported their alarming findings about "The Extent of Crime in the United States."[7] They graphically illustrated the escalation of crime in our nation from 1968 to 1973.[8] The crimes included such categories as: violent crime, crimes against property, forcible rape, and aggravated assault and robbery. No further proof is required to substantiate this nation's moral decay. No further evidence is needed to prove that immediate reforms must be made, particularly in the all-important field of education.

Notes

1. Lou Jacquet, "Our Sunday Visitor," South Bend, Indiana, June 25, 1989, p. 3.
2. Rose L. Martin, *The Selling of America*. Fidelis Publishing

Company, Santa Monica, California: 1973, pp. 68–70.
C. Antonio Provost, *The Sexual Revolution: Its Impact on Society.* Vantage Press, New York, 1985, p. 16.

3. Boris Sokoloff, *The Permissive Society.* Arlington House, New Rochelle, New York, 1972, pp. 5–7.
4. Ibid., pp. 180–207.
5. Peter L. Berger, *Invitation to Sociology.* Doubleday & Company, Garden City, New York, 1963, pp. 168, 169.
6. Ibid., p. 63.
7. Jack Wright, Jr., and James A. Kitchens, *Social Problems in America,* Charles E. Merrill Publishing Company, Columbus, Ohio, 1976, pp. 22–30.
8. Ibid., pp. 27–29.

Chapter II

PHILOSOPHY, PHILOSOPHERS, AND THEIR IMPACT ON SOCIETY

What is philosophy? *Webster's Encyclopedia Dictionary* defines it as: "love of wisdom" and "the science which aims at an explanation of all the phenomena of the universe by ultimate causes; the knowledge of phenomena explained by, and resolved into, causes and reasons, powers and laws; . . . practical wisdom." It deals with causes and effects of complex social problems, but it is more than that because it covers various human behaviors and embraces the combined wisdom gathered throughout the ages.

Since this involves a great deal of mental energy and contemplation, it is little wonder that so few people have ventured into this field of study.

For example, it has been said:

Aristotle is not light reading, but anyone with a taste for pondering over the still unsolved problems of nature and human life will find himself more than rewarded for any effort he may make to understand the thinking of one of the great minds of history.[1]

As a matter of fact, no genuine philosophical treatise can be considered light or frivolous reading; all such works require much mental effort to fully understand the complexities of the problems with which it deals. However we may simplify philosophy, in a world with so many distractions, it takes a real desire for wisdom in order to persevere and enjoy the process of this study.

Wisdom is our heritage; in some instances it is commonplace knowledge, passed on from generation to generation, consciously and unconsciously. However, the tragedy is that much of our accumulated wisdom has been either ignored or rejected by the vast majority of our citizens in recent years.

The enormous task of creating a real *modern renaissance* is not beyond the realm of possibility even though the unwitting enemies of our society wittingly and unwittingly do their utmost to keep it from happening. They revel in their vices and try to induce others to join them in their sort of behavior.

Can we make the study of philosophy a popular pursuit? The optimists are certain that within a decade or two its popularity will grow and literate people will devote more of their leisure time to this invaluable pursuit. Philosophy has the potential to enrich impoverished lives, and guide us along the path of virtue, which leads to peace of soul.

9

As one writer stated a few years ago:

> Modern social institutions, for the most part, are appealing to philosophers more and more for help with moral problems created by modern technology and its role in an ever changing world. . . . Individuals, particularly younger persons appear more willing to examine traditional philosophy that might offer personal values on such subjects as sex and cults, work and dying. . . .[2]

While this might have been true a few years ago, is it true today? Are the younger generations willing to listen and adhere to the judicious principles of the great philosophers? It does not appear to be the case. They are too caught up in the current waves and undertows of dangerous philosophy and sensuous life styles to give much thought to philosophy of the right kind. For the most part, many youths *and* adults have dissipated their energies, thereby lacking the capacity to concentrate. Of course, there are some young students of philosophy and older people, who do recognize its value. They are the main hope for the salvation of our nation and the progress of civilization in general.

The difficulties faced by philosophers such as Socrates, Plato, and Aristotle are well known to those who have studied their lives. Socrates was martyred for his convictions, and both Plato and Aristotle narrowly escaped the adversaries of philosophy. One of Socrates' main admonitions was expressed in these few words: "The unexamined life is not worth living," and in *Phaedo,* "So it is clear first of all that in the case of physical pleasures that the philosopher frees his soul from association with the body, so far as is possible, to a greater extent than other men."[3] He concluded, "In fact, it is wisdom that makes possible courage and self-control and integrity or, in other words, true goodness."[4]

These words are part of the essence of the Socratic dialogues and doctrines, which enabled Plato to contribute to the development of Aristotle and others. The making of such great minds did not happen by chance; both Plato and Aristotle *sought* knowledge; they devoured the wisdom of Socrates, and as a consequence we became the heirs of their classic literature. Their invaluable contributions served to enlighten our culture.

We owe them a debt of gratitude. If we who possess the capacity, however infinitesimal it might appear to be, to promote their judicious doctrines, we should feel duty bound to do what is possible to ensure that civilization will not falter. Our society will prosper far better if their works are made known on a much wider scale.

It seems that the perversity of some human beings has no boundaries; everywhere in our nation there are people who have no use for wisdom; they revel in mediocrity and purely fictional material; they feast on literary garbage that offers meaningless or destructive forms of entertainment. Some authors and publishers feel that it is their right to create and promote anything they wish, notwithstanding the damage their works have done and will do to our society. These philosophical illiterates cannot comprehend why their products are destroying the country and its citizens.

Pornographers flourish, some accumulating vast fortunes as they adversely influence millions who are totally ignorant of what they are doing to themselves by indulging in their various forms of degrading "entertainment." It is the sacred duty of genuine philosophers and sociologists to do what is within their means to help combat such unscrupulous foes of society.

Just as Socrates, Plato, and Aristotle made such a vast difference in helping to combat vice and man's inhumanity to man, so can our well-educated and concerned citizens rise up to rally for the all-important cause of the common good. It is certain that if concerned authors and publishers join the struggle against the forces of evil, ultimately the forces of good will be triumphant. We have much support in this endeavor; we are not alone; we have many who have inspired us to labor incessantly in this nationwide and universal battle.

The following is a succinct summary of part of Plato's basic ethical philosophy:

Plato's ethical theory, like that of other Greek philosophers, is an attempt to answer the question, "What is the good life?" Plato develops the thesis that the life of reason is the happiest and best. For him this means that knowledge produces a harmonious man [woman, boy or girl] in a sense that when reason governs the desires and passions, an orderly and well-balanced personality results.

Indeed, only knowledge can lead to virtue, when a man is ignorant, his personality is disorganized, for the unruly desires and passions [especially when it pertains to sex] then control him. By contrast, when a man truly knows what is good [and the best for his or her maximum development and well being] . . . he is truly happy. . . . In the history of Greek philosophy, Plato stands as a distinguished advocate of the well-rounded life, guided by reason.[5]

It is quite evident that genuine and lasting happiness in which the quality of one's life is at its highest level is attainable. Some kinds of happiness may be of only brief duration. These are not the kinds of happiness to which Plato refers. Some forms of happiness are counterproductive in the lives of those whose happiness or joys are totally without right reason. It is a fleeting kind of bliss with adverse side effects that often result in a disordered personality, a listless and nonproductive life, and in many instances criminal behavior, as in the case of prostitutes and their customers. The role of the philosopher in his arguments for the virtuous lifestyle and against vice is a most vital one.

From the *Great Books* with their abundant "Wisdom of the Western World" and edifying works of philosophers and other authors, we have profitted immensely. By the pursuit of such learning, initially we made a great deal of progress, culturally and sociologically. Now progress has been and is continuing to be severely threatened by unscrupulous authors and producers who are the unwitting arch foes of the civilized world.

We have witnessed the calamity such books as the *Communist Manifesto* and Hitler's *Mein Kampf* have wrought. In our nation, we have writings and other productions which are just as damaging to us.

What might appear to be insurmountable obstacles to combatting such evils in our society can be effectively counteracted. There is genuine philosophy, which if utilized effectively, will enable us to be triumphant over our foes. We need not be discouraged by the enormity of the problems and the strength of our enemies. We need but unite our own well-equipped forces against them in order to make our nation a safer and more tranquil place to live. It is a matter of will.

We need not be concerned about being labeled as prophets of doom when we point out what is happening to our country and where we are headed. We must first recognize evil before we can prescribe the proper remedies. And we must warn against the consequences of not taking appropriate action.

We must expect and work toward creating a "Birth of the Modern Renaissance" which will usher in a genuine rebirth of learning in the highest sense of the word.

This battle against the forces of evil, hedonism, and nihilism which have been dominating our society for so many decades, creating havoc and polluting our social environment, can be won.

When the underlying causes of our steady decay

are clearly understood, the abuses of "Freedom of the Press" and "Free Speech," the corrupting influence of some television programs and degrading forms of literature can be fought and we become victors, not their victims.

The many forms of entertainment which contribute to juvenile *and* adult delinquency will no longer be as popular when the producers are exposed. The question will be asked, "Who are we to judge others? The answer is that we must judge in order to eliminate the evils that affect us.

Philosophers are judges when they consider what is happening to society and humanity; they base their conclusions on what they know is serving the common good and what actions are detrimental to society. Through their studies and observation, analysis and contemplation, they arrive at a formula which is most appropriate for advancing civilization. They feel it is their sacred duty to divulge what they have discovered.

By disclosing the main causes and the consequences of vice, they inform and motivate those who care to take remedial action for the common good. The real philosopher monitors the social climate and fearlessly tells us what he has discovered even if his discoveries may be offensive or displeasing to some segments of the society and therefore rejected or ignored by them.

The urgent need for philosophers to continue to issue the clarion call for immediate action has never been more pronounced than it is today, and there are many who are heeding the call. Thousands of men and women volunteers help shoulder the burden, many making huge sacrifices for the common good. There are some dedicated teachers who are doing their best under very difficult circumstances to inoculate the students against the worst elements in the environment. Pupils who have such teachers are most fortunate. Unfortunately some teachers are a disgrace to the profession and misguide the susceptible young.

The delinquency of some instructors is appalling. Maleducated teachers and professors continue to perpetuate the vicious cycle resulting in an endless chain of social problems.

Philosophical illiteracy is rampant among some of our "educators." One head of a college department confessed that all he knew about Aristotle's work was his *Poetics*—during a discourse in class. With a master's degree, he should have been required to know much more about Aristotle. There is no way of knowing how many Ph.D.s and heads of various departments in our colleges and universities are just as ignorant, but from the evidence in our society, there are many.

Fortunately, even mediocre and poorly trained teachers can learn and develop into the kind of instructors who can set the best examples and motivate and inspire their students to make the most of their potential. But they have to be schooled in the kind of philosophy that will promote such advancement.

To do this, special courses in such philosophy

should be required. At a college forum at MiraCosta College in Oceanside, CA, the philosopher, Mortimer Adler, was asked, "Shouldn't a good knowledge of the works of Plato and Aristotle be required before a doctor of philosophy degree is granted?" He answered unhesitatingly in the affirmative.

It is not only through study of the great philosophers that we can gain a well-rounded, liberal education; some little-known journalists and editors also are influential in enriching our knowledge and bettering our lives. Very good philosophy, especially the homespun variety exists about everywhere in our environment. In the churches and even from TV and radio, occasionally sound philosophy is communicated.

We need not remain the victims of our own inertia or the indifferent majority; we have the ability to change our attitudes and break the vicious cycle.

Those who write inspiring poetry and other equally uplifting works including music, in a certain sense are just as vital to the creation of the *Modern Renaissance*. Poets have inspired philosophers, and many *are* philosophers; the best of classical music also has been a source of inspiration, for it frees and invigorates the soul.

There is a vast wealth of philosophical material stored in some of our homes and all of our libraries—but they have to be utilized.

Socrates, Greek Philosopher and Teacher (470–399 B.C.)

18

Aristotle, Greek Philosopher and Teacher (382–322 B.C.)
Plato, Greek Philosopher, Aristotle's Teacher (427–347
B.C.)

Let us consider the following maxims which contain the wisdom of a few philosophers, poets, statesmen and authors who have inspired many:

... And hence virtue would be, as it were, the health and beauty and harmony of the soul; vice however, disease, and ugliness and weakness.

Plato

... Accordingly, the highest good of man consists in the exercise of the virtue and excellences of the soul, especially of the highest and most perfect.

Aristotle

And therefore, virtue is the good and vice the evil for everyone.

Shaftesbury

He redeemed his vices with his virtues. There was more in him to be praised than to be pardoned.

Ben Johnson, Discoveries

Virtue is persecuted more by the wicked man than it is loved by the good.

Cervantes, Don Quixote

Assume a virtue if you have it not.

Shakespeare, Hamlet

What were once vices are now manners [customs and popular behavior] of the day.

Seneca, Ad Lucilium

Vice is a monster of so frightful mien [a human aspect and behavior], as to be hated needs to be seen; yet seen too often, familiar with her face, we first endure, then pity, then embrace.

Alexander Pope, Essay on Man

A little learning is a dangerous thing;
Drink deeply or taste not the Pierian Spring.

Alexander Pope, An Essay on Criticism

Learning is acquired by reading books; but the much more necessary learning, the knowledge of the world, is only to be acquired by reading men and studying all the various editions of them.

Lord Chesterfield, Letters to his Son

If the American people honored wisdom and goodness as they honor power and success, the system of universal free education would be quite different from what it is today.
Robert M. Hutchins, Wisdom of the Great Books of the Western World

Let us remember that Socrates and Gandhi did not seek to adapt themselves to society as they found it. They attempted to re-make society, and the fact that they died in the attempt in no way detracts from their glory or from their value as an example to other men.

Ibid

Most of the important things that human beings ought to understand cannot be comprehended in youth [but as one matures fully, he gains the capacity to reason and understand what was formerly incomprehensible].

Ibid

I considered my newspaper and the Almanac of 1757 as means on instruction, and published them in extracts

21

from moral writers and little pieces of my own, in the form of Socratic dialogue, tending to prove the advantages of virtue and disadvantages of vice.
Benjamin Franklin, Poor Richard's Rule for Success

Mistakes in business or in science are costly and deplorable, but mistakes in the conduct of [one's] life are usually dangerous to life itself. . . . [It can prove to be fatal.]
Alfred Adler, from the preface to *Understanding Human Nature* (1927)

When we find an individual whose behavior pattern has rendered him incapable of a happy life, there arises out of our knowledge the implicit duty to aid him in readjusting the false perspectives with which he wanders through his life. We must give him better perspectives.

Ibid

This over-swollen stream of indiscriminate books, low in character, vulgar and corrupting, and entertaining the masses, and saturating the mind with distasteful filthiness—is not a blessing but an unmitigated curse. . . . Great books are the key to man's culture. If they vanished and could not be replaced, our civilization would disappear. Great books are a treasure, a precious storehouse. They contain enough to make us rich for all time and eternity.
Leon Gutterman, Wisdom of the Great Books of the Western World

What Gutterman, the editor and publisher of *Wisdom Magazine,* wrote in the sixties about books which are destroying society and the truly great books is just as relevant today. Unfortunately, worse kinds of literature and pornography have inundated book stores and even some public libraries in our nation. The love for great books, the classics, has diminished. No longer are they valued as they were many decades in the past. It is this most alarming trend that worries and baffles the concerned citizens who are well-read and fully understand the nature of our complex social problems and the root causes.

Philosophical illiteracy, the total ignorance of the value inherent in the wisdom contained in the works of humanity's greatest minds, can be seen in the products of many writers and publishers as well as producers in the field of entertainment. They often cater to the lowest elements of our society who are growing each year and in some areas appear to be in the majority. The magnitude of these social problems is quite evident in the daily papers and on TV or radio, particularly the "Talk Shows."

Is it too much to ask our legislators and law enforcement agencies to do far better in enacting and enforcing stronger laws which will curb the root causes of our "social diseases," the crime waves, and delinquency? *They should listen to our pleas.* If they become seriously involved in the study of philosophy, they will certainly better understand the nature of our problems and how to solve them. In coping with our complex interrelated social problems, including the expanding drug addiction, we must consider all of the contributing factors.

Is there a blueprint or formula for bringing about a significant reduction in the chief causes of our social decay? Unfortunately, there is no immediate cure-all, no panacea, no magic formula. But we do know that the understanding and application of the right kind of philosophy holds the keys to some of the solutions.

Philosophers worthy of the name have a huge self-imposed responsibility. If they know that they are philosophers, or even if they have some doubts as to whether they are, if they have accumulated a vast amount of knowledge to which all of us are the heirs, it is incumbent on them to produce and publish their findings in order to help solve our major social problems.

Fortunately, there are philosophers and knowledgeable citizens who are dedicated to this cause. There are those who are willing to publish their own works if necessary. A few philosophers have done exactly that. They found joy in their sacrifices and accomplishments for the common good. They know that other humanitarians and philosophers have in the distant past, at their own expense without expectation of monetary gains, unselfishly devoted the greater part of their works and lives for the benefit of others. Their example has motivated the numerous men and women who also have devoted much of their lives to the benefit of mankind.

By emulating what they have done, to a certain degree, we can contribute toward reaching the ultimate goal, even if our efforts fall short of the works of those extraordinary benefactors of humanity.

What a pleasure it is for those who have added

something of lasting value through their individual efforts for the common good! Indeed! By giving of ourselves, by the sacrifices we willingly make for the sake of those who are less educated and for those countless millions who have been misled, we derive a special kind of happiness, a tranquil bliss that is far different from the fleeting joys of mere sensuality.

As I have noted, it is not only the philosophers who have been greatly instrumental in the advancement of society. Notwithstanding the fact that within the realm of religion there have been much publicized scandalous and unethical activities in recent years, religion remains a vital factor in our culture. It is just as important to discuss it as is philosophy and sociology. Have we not seen or read about saintly men and women in the field of religion who have contributed immensely toward the progress of civilization? With all the faults of those of us who profess a religion, it is inescapable that the values exist and deserve to be considered.

Notes

1. *Aristotle on Man in the Universe* (Edited by Louise Ropes Loomis, Classic Club, Walter J. Black, Inc., Roslyn, New York, 1943, p. xxxvii.
2. Robert C. Toth, *The Los Angeles Times,* "Philosophers Descend the Ivory Tower," 1985.
3. Edith Hamilton and Huntington Cairns, *The Collected Dia-*

logues of Plato, Bollington Series, Princeton University Press, Princeton, New Jersey, 1978.

4. Ibid., pp. 51, 52.
5. Ethel Albert, Theodore C. Denise, and Sheldon P. Peterfreund, *Great Traditions and Ethics,* D. Van Nostrand Co., New York, 1975, p. 11.

Chapter III

RELIGION AND ITS IMPACT ON HUMANITY

What is religion? There are now more than one definition to be certain. In 1844 Karl Marx wrote: "Religion is the opium of the people."[1] Sigmund Freud in his *The Future of an Illusion* (p. 92) said: "Religion is comparable to a childhood neurosis." Other atheists and anti-religionists also have considered religion to be mythology, with little or no value to society, while millions see religion in quite a different light. Religion, defined in a positive and realistic way is: "The feeling of reverence toward a Supreme Being; the recognition of God as an object of worship, love and obedience; piety; any system of faith and worship, e.g., *Natural Religion*—the knowledge of God and of our duty which is derived from the light of nature, or *Revealed Religion*—the knowledge of God and of our duty from positive revelation." Thus, religion encompasses several meanings, but essentially it is a faith in a Supreme Being

27

or a God—the Supernatural. Secondly, it encompasses the practice of a particular faith and allegiance to God and methods of worship.

What have some of our enlightened minds said constructively about religion as a whole? The following is a joint statement by the renowned scientist, Robert A. Millikan (1868-1953), and 14 other distinguished "Men of Affairs," and some religious leaders in the United States.

We, the undersigned deeply regret that in recent controversies there has been a tendency to present science and religion as irreconcilable and antagonistic domains of thought, for in fact they meet distinct human needs and in the rounding out of human life they supplement rather than displace or oppose each other.

The purpose of science is to develop, without prejudice or preconception of any kind, a knowledge of the facts, the laws, and the processes of nature. The even more important task of religion, on the other hand, is to develop the conscience, the ideals, and the aspirations of mankind. Each of these activities represents a deep and vital function of the soul of man, and both are necessary for life, the progress, and happiness of the human race.

It is a sublime conception of God which is furnished by science, and one wholly consonant with the highest ideals of religion, when it represents Him as revealing Himself through countless ages in the development of the earth as an abode for man in the age-long inbreathing of life into its constituent matter, culminating in man with his spiritual nature and all his Godlike powers.[2]

Dr. Millikan added:

Religion and science, in my analysis, are the two great sister forces which have pulled, and are still pulling mankind onward. And the two are necessarily intimately related, for the primary idea in religion lies in the single word "ought". . . .

These quotations reveal the importance they sincerely give to the value of religion.

Such profound statements in the defense of religion signed by illustrious citizens of our country deserves very serious consideration. With all the faults and frailties of those affiliated with some religious organizations, it is nevertheless certain, that without some ethical foundation fostered by religion or philosophy, human behavior would have been much worse.

Some may point out that in various predominantly atheistic countries there appears to be less crime than in our free society. This may be so but in some cases, the leaders rule with an iron hand and never coddle or pamper the criminal elements. Those regimes mete out the most severe and brutal punishment. Justice moves swiftly and little or no mercy is shown to offenders.

In our too free society and with its too lenient treatment in some prisons and correctional institutions, some actually commit more crimes to get back into their "homes" behind bars where they are entertained, clothed, fed, and well housed. Having a "bad reputation" means nothing to them, so they have nothing to lose. Such leniency obviously is not a deterrent to crime. Some convicts are repeatedly paroled even though their habital lawbreaking behavior indicates they are incorrigible criminals. In most cases rehabilitation methods have failed. The excuse given for their release is that we don't have enough prisons or staff.

This is why it is so necessary to have better preventive measures which include exposing all of our citizens and noncitizens to religion at a very early age.

George Washington remarked in his famous farewell address:

> Of all the dispositions and habits which lead to political prosperity, religion and morality are indispensable supports. In vain would that man claim the tribute of patriotism, who should labor to subvert these great pillars of human happiness, these firmest props of the destinies of men and women and all citizens.[3]

It is apparent that we have steadily drifted away from such judicious principles and have carried the concept of "separation of church and state" too far. We have permitted anti-religious forces and militant atheists to dominate the social and political scene.

Sociologists should conduct research in our penal institutions in order to determine the religious education of the inmates. I anticipate that the findings would indicate that the less religious education and church attendance the inmates had received from childhood to adulthood, the greater the incidence of their criminal behavior. If this turns out to be the case, the need for religion would be validated.

The present hue and cry for the total exclusion of religion in our schools will continue in spite of the fact that it is one of the best means of helping people learn self-discipline in all forms of behavior, especially in sexuality. While it is true that some have failed despite their religious training, and allowed themselves to be seduced by peer pressures in an unsuitable environment, most have become law-abiding and constructive contributors to society. No particular denominational approach is required. The statements of our famous scientist, Robert A. Millikan and others of his caliber, if instilled in the minds of students, would encourage them to practice their religion and attend services more often. Through the practice of their religion, numerous men and women have made their talents available for the common good. The anti-religionists and militant atheists would have us ignore or forget what people of various religious denominations have done and continue to do for the common good.

The contributions have been many and include nonprofit hospitals founded and staffed by members of religious faiths, and the homes for the less fortunate.

Another valid testimony to the value and need for information on religion is found in *To Light a Candle* (a Christopher Publication):

. . . American Education and Religion quoted the following extract from a *Jewish Educator's View,* by Simon Greenburg:

"The schools cannot be said to be teaching history at all if they eliminate completely whole areas of human experience. Religion and religious institutions have been determining factors in the evolution of civilization. To omit a study of them in a course of history is to pervert history [and to deny the students invaluable knowledge]."[4]

Notes

1. Karl Marx, *Introduction to a Critique of the Hegelian Philosophy of Right.*
2. Robert A. Millikan, *The Autobiography of Robert A. Millikan.* New York: Prentice-Hall, 1950, p. 239.
3. Henry C. Link, *The Return to Religion,* MacMillan Company, New York, pp. 104–105.
4. James Keller, *To Light A Candle,* The Autobiography of James Keller (Founder of the Christophers), Doubleday and Company, Garden City, New York, 1963, p. 207.

Chapter IV

EDUCATION: ITS DEFECTS
AND MEANS OF REFORM

The reviewer of D. Bob Gowin's book, *Educating,* states:

> Although education has been the subject of numerous books, articles and studies, most have either been glorified journalism or an attempt to treat education as just another area in which to apply the technique of history, sociology, psychology, philosophy or what have you. Few works treated education on its own terms. . . . This preferred definition is: "Educating as an eventual process, changing the meaning of human experience by intervention in the lives of people with meaningful materials to develop thinking, feeling, and acting as habitual dispositions in order to make of human experience by using appropriate criteria of excellence."[1]

This comprehensive definition of educating and of education encompasses a full range of meanings, but the core appears to be "the intervention in the lives of people with meaningful materials" and also "to develop thinking." If education fails to include the essentials for proper behavior, it is not really adequate and falls far short of what education should be. Students are being cheated by the deficiencies in education, and we can no longer tolerate this condition.

Ancient philosophers and some modern philosophers have attempted to achieve the above goals. By their *"intervention" in the lives of people,* they have not only been successful in contributing toward the advancement not only of individuals who have appreciated and fully utilized their philosophy, but they have contributed immensely toward the progress of civilization. In light of Godwin's definition, the failure of our educators to design the process over the past few decades is evident. Of course there are some exceptions. A few have done great work in formulating curricula which are in compliance with the highest principles of education. But in general, what Godwin and other critics of our system of education have been saying appears to be quite valid.

What further proof do we need than what our educational system as a whole has been able to produce during the past forty or fifty years? Has there been a rise in scholarship and scientific or social achievements, or has there been a steady decline? Has literacy increased or decreased? The answers are quite obvious to those who have studied the statistics. Genuine literacy on such vital subjects as philosophy and sociology has declined as well as in other areas, and the value of religion for the most part has not

34

even been considered as being important for the common good. For this main reason, reform in education is of paramount importance. It should be our number one priority.

To accomplish such reform, every suggestion for revitalizing and improving our educational system that is feasible, should be applied in order to make our nation more livable, productive, and crime free. We know what happens when a population has little or no formal education or is maleducated. One extreme example in some uncivilized societies, is or was cannibalism. Another is the use of witch doctors. Some poorly educated people in our own nation subscribe to customs or behaviors that are not much different from those of uncivilized tribes and savages. But do we really know the root causes of uncivilized behaviors in our very midst?

Professor Allan Bloom has written the most profound critique of "higher education." His astute analysis of the academic world is most timely and valid:

The humanities are the specialty that now exclusively possesses the books that are not specialized, that insists upon asking about the whole that are excluded from the rest of the university, which is dominated by real specialists, as resistant to self-examination as they were in Socrates' day and now rid of the gadfly. The humanities have not had the vigor to fight it out with triumphant natural science, and want to act as though it were just a specialty. But as I have said over and over again, however much the humane disciplines would like to forget about their essential conflict with natural science as now practiced and understood, they are gradually undermined by it. . . . Natural science asserts that it is metaphysically neutral, and hence has no need for philosophy. . . .[2]

It is the natural science departments and anti-philosophy professors as well as some philosophy professors themselves, that place us at odds with the judicious doctrines of the greatest of all philosophers. Bloom's profound assessment is relevant and disturbing to many other educators and students in the field.

The widespread animosity toward genuine philosophy, the disinclination to introduce some elementary philosophy courses in the lower levels of education, is certainly one of the root causes of the intellectual anemia and mental stagnation of so large a number of college and university graduates. Some philosophy courses should be mandatory from high school through university programs.

If only half of Professor Bloom's recommendations were introduced in our schools, it would not be very long before we would see the necessary reforms. The validity of most of his conclusions cannot be refuted. Through personal experience and research in the academic world, he has come to understand the true nature of our educational institutions.

The professors of philosophy and educators could very well stand a "refresher course" in philosophy, and Professor Bloom's book would be a fitting text. Although some of his ideas and criticism may disturb many, they would learn a great deal that would be of benefit to themselves and to society. In addition, a review of Plato's *Republic* and his *Laws,* and Aristotle's works, especially his treatise, *Nicomachean Ethics,* would enable educators to devise curricula which would reflect their wisdom. Simplified versions of such courses introduced in the grade schools would be invaluable in laying the groundwork for future applications of the constructive ideas presented.

In addition to reforming the curriculum, the use of appropriate role models is of utmost importance. We must counteract the deleterious effect of the "bad" role models presented in the media as noted earlier. Among the many who have exemplified the most constructive role models are George Washington Carver (1864–1943) and Helen Keller (1819–1890), two people who surmounted severe obstacles and achieved greatness.

George Washington Carver, the son of a slave woman, despite his lowly beginnings, achieved fame as an educator, a botanist, an agricultural chemist and researcher, and as an artist of above average talent. How many students have been made aware of this great man and his achievements? How many know of the awards and prizes he received such as his election as Fellow of the Royal Society of Arts in Great Britain[3] and the Springarm Medal for distinguished research in agriculture chemistry?[4]

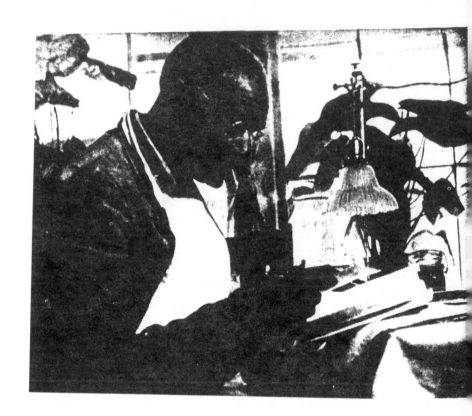

George Washington Carver

Scientist, Artist, and Teacher (1864-1943)
(Photo courtesy Tuskegee Institute, Alabama)

A ROLE MODEL

Helen Keller

Author and Lecturer (1919-1890)
(Courtesy the Library of Congress)

He later received an honorary Doctor of Science degree from Simpson College. And there is no doubt that he would have received more recognition and higher honors if not for the racial prejudices and discrimination of the time.

What were some of the factors in his education which were largely responsible for his remarkable development? Religion was one. It played a vital part in his early childhood education: "He was permitted to attend Sabbath school class which was held before the church services. . . ." For another, he worked his way through high school doing odd jobs. Throughout his college career, he was very studious, especially in the fields of agricultural and chemistry. He "was greatly in demand as a lecturer . . . the important duty of advancing agriculture could not be confined to Tuskegee Institute which he founded, and to its environs alone."[5] He was the author of many scientific articles that were widely published.

Professor Carver's firm religious conviction was evident when he said "You must either take heed of the Bible . . . or if you thought it all bush, throw it away." "He chose to take heed."[6]

There is no doubt that his religious upbringing and strong application to learning were the main sources of his self-discipline and character development. Most unfortunately these ingredients are sorely lacking in our public schools and in some institutions of higher learning.

Helen Keller was stricken with a disease which resulted in her becoming totally blind and deaf when she was 19 months old. Such handicaps would be insurmountable for most people, but she overcame them to achieve fame as a lecturer and author. At age seventeen, she became an art student and quickly learned to read and to type, beginning her writing career shortly after her special education. She later served on the Massachusetts Commission for the Blind.

In her life as well, religion played a vital part. She said, "Thank God for my handicaps for through them I have found myself, my work, and my God."[7] It is this source of inspiration which is lacking in most schools today. Its omission creates a vacuum, an emptiness, and sometimes a hopelessness in so many lives. One does not have to teach a specific religion in our public schools, but not to teach the value of religion is to deprive students of an understanding of the merits of all our major constructive religions. For a liberal education to be truly liberal and not anti-religious, all students must be informed of the inherent value of religion.

Helen Keller, deprived of sight and hearing, received much instruction in religion and the Bible.[8] Thus, she found strength through her faith. "*The Story of My Life* . . . published in 1902 while she was still in Radcliffe, confirmed her international reputation of growing greatness. *The Story of My Life* promptly became a classic. It is published in some fifty languages and seldom out of print."[9]

THE ROLE MODELS

Why are positive role models so important, especially to the young? From early childhood people tend to emulate their heroes or at least those life styles they find attractive. Thus, there is the need to offer the best kind of role models starting with parents and teachers. Among the best role models are those who were or are handicapped, either physically, socially or economically and were able to overcome their disabilities. There are thousands of other handicapped men and women besides the two described here who have demonstrated what it requires to excel in one or more fields of endeavor. Thus, the value of introducing a course of study in our schools based on the biographies of the most outstanding achievers seems obvious. Because role models are so important, such a class should be mandatory. The syllabus should include the requirement that students read at least ten biographies of famous men and women of untarnished character. George Washington Carver and Helen Keller are ideal examples of such people.

Students would be required to answer the following questions:

1. Why did you select your particular role models?
2. How were handicapped people able to achieve success?
3. To what did they attribute their development and character formation?
4. What were their major goals?

5. What literature did they read?
6. When did they first start to strive toward achieving their goals?
7. Which one would you like to use as your best role model and why?
8. What should you avoid, as they have done, in order to make the most of your potential?
9. What was the most important factor they attributed to their success during their childhood and teenage years?
10. What were some of the sacrifices they made in order to achieve their major goals?

Such a "Role Model Class" would increase the school's potential for producing more scholarly students, and reduce delinquency. They would realize what the best kind of value system had done for the role models and how their principles and philosophy could become factors for their own enrichment. No student would be allowed to graduate unless he took the course and received a passing grade.

If handicapped role models are able to accomplish so much, it appears that those of us without serious handicaps should be at least able to become creative and productive to some degree. This kind of a course can be implemented with a minimum of effort and expense. The enormous rewards for this addition to the curricula in most of our elementary and high schools (mid schools), is apparent. The teachers are overburdened with discipline problems; they would see them decreasing as the exemplary lives of the role model begins to take effect on them as students become more goal-oriented at the elementary grade level.

The people who are best qualified to institute the necessary changes and to introduce the best kinds of courses are those who are well versed in philosophy and sociology. But they should be tested to make certain that they have earned their degrees and fully understand the chief works of Plato and Aristotle and others of that caliber.

Many dropouts and delinquencies result from a lack of knowledge of ethics and the fundamental principles of philosophy. Peer pressure by the worst elements as well as a destructive educational and social environment lead many astray. Under the adverse influences, some resort to harmful drugs and dangerous habits to fill the emptiness in their souls. Many become incorrigible and turn to various criminal activities—all because of maleducation, all because of the deficiencies in our system and the faulty curricula nationwide. The implications are evident.

Even some of our teachers show signs of their delinquency and at times contribute to that of their students. They create a vicious cycle—delinquent teachers help make delinquent students who become parents and teachers, who in turn produce more delinquent students. The teaching in the homes in some cases breeds delinquency. Indeed, proper education is vitally important. The *status quo* must go. We must immediately help to bring about the necessary changes in our society. *The longer we pro-*

crastinate in instituting measures of reform, the worse our problems will grow.

It is important to the students as well as those who are no longer in the institutions of learning to understand "that the greatest mistake anyone can make about liberal education is to suppose that it can be acquired, once and for all, in the course of one's youth and by [merely] passing through school or college."[10]

Adler's views on the reading of *Great Books* exemplifies "educating" at its very best; he motivates the readers to drink deeply from the fountains of knowledge and to explore worlds of wisdom in order to improve the quality of our lives. His book on Aristotle[12] deserves a place in every public school and private library and curriculum. Such an addition to the curricula would enhance the students' preparedness to succeed in becoming citizens of the highest caliber. Superior scholars and motivators of others not in school would therefore be developed.

Such books would be most valuable especially in the first year in the middle schools. Students would learn to think properly at an early age and thus avoid the seduction of inferior books. It would ensure that they continue their education in and out of our school throughout their entire lives. Such reform in educating has far-reaching constructive implications for the creation of a far more civilized and advanced society. Philosopher Adler wrote about "productive thinking" and "means and ends"[13] for reaching goals.

The most damaging evidence and testimony against public education over the past two to three decades are provided by some educators themselves. Books they have published give detailed information about some of the defects in our system.[14] Author Dan C. Alexander, Jr. revealed the findings of The National Commission on Excellence in Education Report of August 1981.[15] The alarming discovery that we are indeed "A Nation at Risk," as the eighteen-month report was termed, included among several other deficiencies, the fact that educational skills were declining, and the "College Board's Scholastic Aptitude Tests (SAT) demonstrated a virtually unbroken decline from 1963 to 1980. Average verbal scores fell over 50 points, and average mathematic scores dropped nearly 40 points."[16]

Some of the main causes of these problems in our educational institutions have already been noted. Poorly educated teachers and deficient curricula produce inferior products. Many of them, in turn, become teachers. It should be obvious what has to be done in order to make significant progress in the field of public education, and there is no doubt that some defects also exist in many nonpublic schools.

In order to produce much better students in general and more superior teachers, the prescription (which may not be palatable to some people) has been offered here. It will not be expensive, and there will be no harmful side effects. All it takes is new textbooks and better teachers.

Before proceeding to the next chapter let us consider the *vast importance of "holistic education"* clearly delineated in the book, *Prometheus Reborn.* The author stated:

> Holistic education is the development of comprehensive awareness. . . . We must learn to be aware of it as a totality, to be aware of the multifold [multifaceted] character of human culture and the community as a whole.[17]

Such is the nature of a well-rounded liberal education; essentially it is the acquiring of the basic knowledge of the humanistic disciplines and the fundamental principles—something very lacking in most of our educational institutions. Through a holistic kind of education we can gain a far better understanding of the nature of our social problems and we can become more capable of finding viable solutions to some of our complex problems.

Notes

1. Robert J. Silverman (Editor), "The Journal of Higher Education," Vol. 54, No. 2, Ohio University Press, March/April 1983, pp. 204–205.
2. Allan Bloom, *The Closing of the American Mind,* Simon and Schuster, New York, 1987, p. 372.
3. Rackham, Holt, *George Washington Carver,* Doubleday & Company, Garden City, New York, 1943, p. 200.
4. Ibid., p. 275.
5. Ibid., p. 200.
6. Ibid., p. 339–340.
7. Richard Harrity and Ralph G. Martin, *The Three Lives of*

Helen Keller. Doubleday and Company, Garden City, New York, 1962, p. 7.

8. Ibid., p. 10, 23.
9. Ibid., p. 65.
10. *Wisdom of the Great Books of the Western World,* "Wisdom Magazine" (Reprint of first issue), 1960, p. 15. (out of print).
11. Ibid.
12. Mortimer J. Adler, *Aristotle for Everybody,* Bantam Books, New York, 1978.
13. Ibid., pp. 64, 65.
14. Dan C. Alexander, Jr., *Who's Ruining Our Schools,* Save Our Schools Research and Education Foundation, Washington, D.C.; 1986; and Max Rafferty, *Suffer Little Children,* The Devin-Adair Company, New York, 1962. Max Rafferty, *What Are They Doing to Our Children,* New American Library, New York, 1963.
15. Dan C. Alexander, Jr., *Who's Ruining Our Schools,* 1986, p. 4.
16. Ibid., p. 5.
17. Michael L. Johnson, *Prometheus Reborn,* Libra Publishers, San Diego, CA, 1977, p. 17.

Chapter V

HUMAN SEXUALITY—
THE PROBLEMS AND SOLUTIONS

"... I believe the decline in moral standards all around us has such a core of evil, I think it lies in our obsession with—and misuse of—sex. Sex is a topic of universal interest, but around it swirl such emotions and prejudices that a sane and balanced discussion of it is rare, to say the least."[1]   *Dr. Norman Vincent Peale*

At no time in the history of humanity have we been faced with such enormous problems in this area of human behavior—problems which require all our ingenuity to find solutions. It is a subject that many people either ignore or refuse to discuss because it is so emotionally charged.

It is not a subject for those who are too timid or prudish to hear or read about some of the most sordid sexual behavior and unethical practices. Nevertheless, it must be discussed if we are to succeed in finding valid solutions. It is quite understandable that people who have established a sexual behavior

49

pattern over a long period of time will never be convinced that another kind of sexual behavior is better. Nevertheless, as Dr. Peale suggests, it should be discussed intelligently.[2]

The following describes what has happened during the *Sexual Revolution* which some "experts" in the field deny, even though in the last four or five decades we have seen the steady decline in sexual morality and an increasing number of sexual perversions and the crimes related to them. We have witnessed television programs in which the sordid details of prostitution and its promotion are depicted as never before. We have read about all kinds of sexual promiscuity and of sexual abuse of children never imagined before. Explicit sex and pornography not suited for the young *or* old have increased. X-rated video cassettes have been introduced and are multiplying.

Indeed there has been a *Sexual Revolution* and it is still growing. A counter-sexual revolution is long overdue.

The *Playboy, Hustler, Screw* and other obnoxious publications, are among the main causes of our social problems and the decay of society. Also, some very questionable talk and other TV shows and some types of courses in sex education in our schools and colleges add to the complexity of the problem.

How can we reverse these unhealthy trends? How can we who are the most concerned make a difference? Can we devise remedies to counteract the works of these unwitting foes of society? Is it possible to reduce man's perversity?

There are no easy answers to these questions, but some organizations and many individuals are trying. One such organization is the *Children's Legal Foundation* (CLF), formerly the *Citizens for Decent Literature* (CDL).

This CLF national organization has published reports of its activities as well as revelations about the social climate of unethical and criminal activities in the area of human sexual behavior.[3] Whatever we are able to do in support of such worthy, patriotic, nonprofit organizations will be greatly appreciated by all concerned citizens in our threatened country.

The extent of seductive sexual materials has increased to alarming proportions. While the publishers of this trash reap fortunes, they contribute to the delinquency of both the young and the "educated" adults who purchase their products.

In addition to supporting organizations such as the CLF, we can begin to promote courses in sexual education which contain the proper ethical perspectives of the greatest philosophers. Many philosophers and great thinkers—ancient, modern, and contemporary—are unanimous in their conclusions as to the adverse effects of the unbridled sex life which is now so prevalent.

One of the most interesting, meaningful, and somewhat humorous discussions can be found in Plato's Socratic dialogue with his students:[4]

Plato: Then tell me, in which case would a man find it an easier task to abstain from sexual gratifications and obey orders on the matter readily, as a decent man should—if his physique were in good condition—in training, in fact—or if it were in poor form?

Clinias (a student): If he were in training, of course. Most decidedly so.

Plato: Well, we have all heard, have we not, how Incus of Tarentum is said to have acted for the sake of distinction at Olympia and elsewhere? Such was his passion for victory, his pride in his calling, the combined fortitude and self-command of his character, as the story goes, that all the time, he never once came near a woman, or a boy either, all the time he was in training. And you know the same is said of Crison, Astylus, Diopompus, and not a few others. And after all, Clinias, they had much worse cultivated minds than the citizens for whom you and I are providing, and much more rebellious bodies.

Clinias: You are perfectly right when you say that tradition asserts this emphatically as actual fact about these athletes.

Plato: Why then, they made no hardship of denying themselves this "heavenly bliss," as the vulgar account in, for the sake of winning a victory in the ring, or on the racecourse, or the like, and are our pupils to fail in endurance for the sake of a far nobler victory?

Clinias: And what victory is that?

Plato: The conquest of their lust. If they achieve it, we shall tell them, their life will be bliss, if they fail [in adequately controlling their sexual appetite], the very reverse.[2]

This dialogue from his Laws (VIII) clearly indicates how strongly he felt about the danger of unbridled lust and the value of sublimation—how important it is for the enrichment of the soul.

Aristotle also referred to this vital topic:

When it comes to a particular or private pleasusre, many a man goes wrong, and he goes wrong in a number of ways. If he is what people call an "addict" to something, it is either because he feels the pleasure more intensely than other people or in a wrong fashion. The intemperate man, indeed goes to excess in all these directions at once, even abominable things. . . . He carried it too far and feels it more intensely than the average man. . . . The intemperate man deliberately chooses to follow in the train of his lusts from a belief that he ought always to pursue the pleasure of the moment . . . [and never tries to control the sexual appetite].[5]

Aristotle's views are quite in accord with his teacher, Plato and his teacher, Socrates. Their philosophy finds company among many other philosophers who fully shared their astute opinions. In his *Nicomachean Ethics* from which the above is quoted, there is much more on temperance in this area of human activity and about the nature of the vices related to it.

An early nineteenth century philosopher, Professor Friedrich Paulsen, added this to the arguments:

A life on the other hand, in which the vegetative and animal functions, sensuous desires and blind passions have control, must be regarded as a lower or abnormal form. A perfect life is a life in which the mind attains a free and full growth and in which the spiritual forces reach their highest perfection in thought, imagination and action . . . the tendency to go to the other extreme is natural and universal; incontinence [inadequate sexual self-control], causes the ruin of many. Excessive temperance, therefore, does not seem to be dangerous, but meritorious . . . and absolute continence [total abstinence] is indirectly meritorious insofar as it shows by great and striking examples, that impulses which often lead to ruinous excesses, assume a form of admiration."

Professor Philosopher Paulsen concluded:

Whenever the organs for procreation are used solely and indiscriminately and as instruments of pleasure excessively, nature punishes the abuse with disturbances and disease, and in case her hints are not followed [or seriously considered], with the destruction of the organs and ultimately of the individual who persists in misunderstanding their true purpose.[6]

Dr. Boris Sokoloff, M.D., Ph.D., described his views on the problems related to human sexuality and the present trends:

An extreme permissiveness of an almost pathological nature, has engulfed a considerable part of the American population, not unlike a fast-growing cancer. Applauded, promoted, fully approved by the liberal intellectuals, the permissive movement was declared by them as a social revolution, as the beginning of a new American life. . . . Uncontrolled freedom of sex reached national proportions, with a growing and dangerous epidemic of venereal diseases. . . . I decided to write this book, telling how a biologist sees the causes of the extreme permissiveness which affects our society and what physiological and biological factors are involved in it. . . . The facts speaks for themselves. . . . It is in the field of sexuality that the influence of the permissiveness of our society is interwoven with pornography and obscenity in this country.[7]

Dr. Sokoloff's most serious indictment of our society and the contributors to its decay, unfortunately, has not resulted in any improvement of the sexual climate, even though it has been over eighteen years since he published his findings. His admonitions for the good of our nation have been ignored. In his chapter on "Sex in America"[8] he revealed the nature of sexual problems as he saw them and the awful trends which have grown much worse in recent years.

Even before these findings, another author produced a treatise on our sociological retrogression. His pleas for reforms also have been unheeded, as have many others' cries for the reconstruction of the social order. The educator, E. H. Staffelback, alerted us to the inherent dangers in our society with which we are still faced:

Great people of the past proved unequal to the task of controlling conditions basic to their survival. Athens, having in early vigor invented a pure form of democracy, and in her prime having nurtured genius in every area of achievement, rotted inwardly, and all of her philosophy could not save her. Rome's ailments were similar. . . . Our best hope—in truth, our one hope—of creating a successful future for our nation, lies in frankly admitting our problems for what they are, and attacking them basically in their entirety. . . . It *will* require of us, and our oncoming youths, submission to self-controls dictated by common sense interpretations of moral wisdom.[9]

Such philosophy denotes the urgent necessity for sexual self-control, an admission that there has been far too much permissiveness and wanton sexual freedom. Such conditions have to be controlled if we are to avoid the tragic fate of other nations which "rotted inwardly."

In the treatises pertaining to "Sexual Ethics," there is moral wisdom which, if correctly interpreted and applied, will bring our social problems to lasting solutions. If the majority of people continue to ignore the warnings and take no remedial action, not much can be accomplished. Thus, the urgent need for the too silent minority to speak out and accept the responsibility to join the forces that are striving desperately to bring about the necessary changes for the common good.

It has been very well stated:

Certainly those who effect great revolutions are always small in numbers. Such people need not wait to become a majority. No one else can do the job except those who understand what needs to be done. The price for such individual action is likely to be high. In Emerson's words, "God offers to every mind its choice between truth and repose. Take which you please—you can never have both."

Never was that choice more clearly presented than in America of the 1970s.[10]

Indeed we must be forever vigilant to ensure that the truth prevails.

It is a matter of recorded history that it take only one or two men to bring about momentous revolutions, much to the destruction of nations and innocent people. Conversely, one or just a few people are capable or rising to the occasion and through their humanitarian efforts, help to bring about constructive social change for the betterment of our nation. Fortunately, there are volunteers who can be depended on to give their services for this truly great universal and national cause.

Dr. Max Rafferty, a prominent official and educator, seeking reforms in the California school system, was deposed mainly because he was opposed to the liberals' view of what sex education should be and what kinds of books were suitable for children in the lower grades. He described the problems he faced when he voiced his opinion that was contrary to the views of the very vocal majority.

A recently published reference book falls right into this trend toward the setting of standards by means of public opinion [or the findings through popular questionnaires by researchers] by dutifully concerning itself with defining in considerable detail the various postures and techniques of sexual perversion. I managed to get into quite a hassle in my home state by venturing to state mildly that I thought this book might possibly be out of place on the shelves of our public libraries and in the hands of our fourteen-year-olds, though certainly suitable for researchers along the lines followed by the late Dr. Kinsey. Almost at once, the disciples of the lowest common denominator fell upon me with anguished cries of "witch hunting" and "book burning" as though I was subverting the foundations of the republic by hinting that some books were not suitable for children. The fact that the book in question dealt with incredible filth was considered unimportant. After all, the argument ran, people do speak this way and think this way, don't they? So what's wrong with putting it all in a reference book for children? To one who has spent his entire life trying to persuade children to think, write and speak in a higher—not lower—frame of reference, this point of view is incomprehensible.[11]

Dr. Rafferty's startling experience, even though he was a prominent head official, is likely to occur when others who strive to institute reasonable, constructive reforms in the school system. Those who might suggest that the present sex education courses and texts need to be revised and/or replaced with those which contain ethical principles, and recommend the restriction or the exclusion of the "sex mechanics" from school books, will be met with the same condemnation.

It is understandable that in the present sexual climate, not many reformers will find the task an easy one.

Dr. Rafferty was attacked and lost his bid for re-election largely because he was courageous enough to take a stand against literature that he felt was harmful to children. He lost because those united against him were delinquents in the field of education.

As I have stressed, what is missing in sex education in general are the findings of judicious philosophy on this vital subject. There are also other findings that are somewhat more physiological and psychological. Some findings on sublimation need to be introduced in this discussion. In addition, there are some theories which are well-supported by empirical data and testimony of doctors and authors in the fields of science and sociology. This information is seldom if ever seen in current books on human sexual activities. This "sin of omission" by educators can be forgiven, for most of them either have no knowledge of the findings or have been misled as to their validity.

The scientist, Dr. Alexis Carrel (1873–1944), winner of the Nobel Prize in 1912 and other major awards, stated:

> It is well known that sexual excesses impede intellectual activity. In order to reach its full power, intelligence seems to require both the presence of well-developed sexual glands and the temporary repression of the sexual appetite. . . .[12]

Many authors fully agree with Dr. Carrel, and have given a more thorough explanation of how sublimation and the conservation of sexual energy is a factor in one's maximum development. Often by personal experience and self-analysis people make the

59

discovery that long periods of voluntary or complete abstinence from erotic activities has the effect of enhancing the powers of the mind as well as increasing physical stamina. Several other authors have testified in support of this controversial concept in spite of the fact that some extraordinary people, highly endowed hereditarily, have been able to display remarkable talents and productivity while dissipating much of their energies. This finding is deceptive since it fails to take into account that with proper restraint they could have achieved much more.

It appears certain that one's potential is reduced in proportion to the degree of overindulgence in sexual activities; conversely, sublimation maximizes creative potential.

In the book, *Think and Grow Rich,* the above phenomenon is explained in some detail. I have also attempted to delineate the process in my book about *The Sexual Revolution.* Other authors have discussed this important matter and have presented evidence in support of their conclusions.

On sublimation, which he terms "sex transmutation," very briefly summarized, Napoleon Hill stated:

The road to genius consists of the development, control, and use of sex, love and romance. . . . The secret of control lies in understanding the process of transmutation [the process of *sublimation*]. . . . Between the ages of thirty and forty, man begins to learn (if he ever learns) the art of sex transmutation. This discovery is generally accidental, and more often than otherwise, the man who makes it is totally unconscious of his discovery that the inherent potential for creativity and increased productivity lies within the sphere of human sexuality and how well we govern and ["transmute" the energies to non-sexual channels].[13]

How soon and how well we apply this mysterious store of energy, can determine the degree of success or failure, creativity or lack of creativity in our lives. We rob ourselves of our potential if we do not pay heed to this finding.

Another book worth mentioning which describes how some people improved the quality of their lives and became more successful, is *The New Celibacy*.[14]

Sublimation, a word not found in the two latest books on the subject of sexuality by Dr. Wardell B. Pomeroy, the co-author of the "famous books" on "Human Sexual Behavior." He has ridiculed the principles. The recommendation in some other books also contain an entirely different perspective.[15]

Pomeroy's two books, directed to boys and girls, condone masturbation and various forms of sexual perversions while belittling sexual and religious ethics of almost all religious institutions.

One can find many other authors whose perspectives are similar. Dr. Winifred Richmond has disagreed with the stand taken by these writers and "social scientists.":

Sublimation as used by psychoanalysis has to do largely with the energy of the sexual impulse, a great part of which must be turned aside from purely sexual activities if the individual is to function [constructively and crea-

61

tively] in any modern society. When energy is used in creative work or play into which the individual can pour a real passionate interest, we have the most effective sublimation . . . it is probable that the majority are capable of much more sublimation of their sexual desires than they ever attain.[16]

It is quite obvious that authors such as Dr. Richmond would conclude that *sublimation instead of masturbation is by far the best and proper course of action when one seeks to reduce the tension of the sex drive, or for sheer pleasure.* Instead of having a negative behavioral impact, the converted sex drive can add to one's potential for productivity and creativity. (It also increases one's capacity to engage in and to enjoy noncarnal forms of pleasure—intellectual and spiritual.)

To suggest that masturbation is or should be the norm, that it should be taught as being an invaluable asset instead of a liability, does an immense disservice to individuals and society.

This controversial topic of masturbation, a practice which has the blessings of the famous Dr. Karl Menninger[17] and others of national prominence in the world of medicine, needs to be fully discussed. He, as well as others in psychiatry and education, can see "no harm" in this habit; "no evil in it." They fully approve of the habit.

It would be an act of cowardice to sidestep the issue or avoid opposing the distinguished doctor's conclusions merely because of his prestige and otherwise constructive contributions. Many people fully realize how important it is to have a "second opinion" when an issue is in doubt. Apart from the religious perspective, *the habit of masturbation is wrong mainly because it often results in a waste of energy; it is wrong because in many cases it tends to make the young sexually precocious and sometimes sexually delinquent; it is wrong because it tends to focus the mind of the child prematurely on sex during a time of his gradual maturation.*

Masturbation is not the intelligent or productive way to learn to handle the sex drive. The mind is capable of controlling it by concentrating on other subjects and activities. The tension can be gradually reduced by the bio-feedback technique (*Readings in Psychology,* 77/78, pp. 60–64 describes "Biofeedback: An Exercise in Self-Control"), which far too few people know about.

Intense study of difficult subject matter, such as profound philosophy or some other discipline which calls for deep concentration is a productive way of harnessing the sexual drive. This transference of potential energy to the brain in particular, is done frequently by most people, consciously and unconsciously, which is why it is called sublimation—the conversion of one form of energy to another.

Why masturbate when one can do far better? This widely condoned practice has cost many people the opportunity to make the most of their potential because they have been convinced that there is no harm in the habit.

It may take a long time to effectively counteract

the misinformation that is so widespread in our country. Thousands of books written over the past forty years support this misguided view.

I do not support the myth that people can "go insane" from masturbation or that it causes dangerous diseases. What I and others firmly believe is that it is a negative factor in one's development. Experiments with biofeedback have demonstrated that this comparatively new technique has immense value. It can remedy some ailments and predispositions. According to the *Merriam-Webster Dictionary,* it is: The technique of making conscious or involuntary bodily processes (as heartbeat or brain waves) objectively perceptible to the senses . . . in order to manifest them by conscious mental control.

Dr. Herbert Benson and others have written a great deal about this technique:

> We have long been aware that man's skeletal muscles are commanded by voluntary nerves acting through the brain. However, Western man has only recently recognized that he can control his involuntary processes such as blood pressure, heart beat, and the amount of blood flow to various parts of the body [which] is called the automatic nervous system. Visceral learning, or biofeedback, as it is popularly called, established that man could control his involuntary or automatic nervous system.[18]

Readings in Psychology (77/78) provides a detailed summary:

> Biofeedback: An Exercise in "Self-Control." The simplest statement of the discovery is revolutionary: Given infor-

mation about how any one of the internal physiological systems is operating, the ordinary human being can learn to control the activity of the system. It can be heartbeat . . . or bits of muscle tissue; it does not seem to make much difference what function of the body it is as long as information about how it is behaving is made available. And generally, the more information, the easier it is to learn to control the body function.[19]

Barbara Brown, a contributor to the publication, continued:

The excitement that biofeedback has brought is the discovery that man's mind can process and understand even its own cellular information and use it to extend his control of self far beyond that ever believed possible.[20]

The unexpectedness of the biofeedback phenomenon stimulates more philosophic scientific conjecture than does any previous psychophysiologic research.

Biofeedback has been successful in an unbelievable array of problems of health: tension and migraine headaches, cardiac irregularities, high blood pressure, peripheral vascular disease, gastric ulcer, insomnia, epilepsy, asthma, spastics . . . a host of other troublesome medical and psychological problems of human beings.[21]

(For a more thorough understanding of biofeedback, I suggest a study of the entire article by the author. Other more recent books and articles no doubt will have more definitive findings).

Thus, *the adequate employment of the psychophysiological principles of biofeedback should be of great help in ultimately controlling sexual impulses.* This process will be easier to apply for some people than for others. However, the infantile habit of masturbation which is condoned by so many, even among the "highly educated" will no longer be acceptable. This *viable alternative will control the impulse and eliminate the inherent tension.*

Lack of self-control of the sexual impulses is the major cause of family disintegration and resultant decay of society. It follows then that including the principles of biofeedback in sex education classes would be most beneficial. Obviously, the stronger the motivation to learn the technique in order to develop self-discipline in this all-important area of human behavior, the more successful it will be.

Conversely, those who are strongly motivated to indulge in erotic activities, will have greater difficulty in mastering biofeedback techniques. This is the main reason why all kinds of pornography is such an evil in our society because it promotes excessive sexual activities and perversions which are dehumanizing.

A case study of a Dominican native, age 33, involving masturbation and approved child molestation in his sub-culture, appeared in a book on mental health. The topic heading was: *Juan Torres—Case Study of Community Mental Health in Context.*[22]

The researcher studied the boy's history from his early childhood environment to his life in the slum neighborhood of New York City where he settled in his adulthood. It was discovered that he had some strange mental and physical problems. One of the factors which appears to have been instrumental in his maladjustment and a probable cause (among others) of his unhealthy mental state, was his childhood and adolescent environment. Although there was no direct evidence of a masturbation addiction, the researcher indicated there might have been, and that the environment was a factor.

> Little boys are permitted to run nude, or wear only a shirt. Adults comment on and may fondle the genitals of the male child and joke about his forthcoming manliness. His own fondling [masturbation] of his genitals is not reproved. Adults admire and reward any tendency to astuteness in the little boy.[23]

That is the subculture in which he was raised—one which we see to a certain extent in our own country, but not generally approved in the mainstream of our society. (It can be conjectured that this is one of the many causes of the pitiful conditions which prevail in the underdeveloped countries and among the very poorly educated population right here in America.) In our slum areas there is "free sex" and very little discipline in matters pertaining to sexual behavior (sexual child abuse is somewhat accepted as the norm). This kind of subculture activity, unfortunately, is condoned by some of our most highly educated citizens. They, too, see no harm in the forming of such infantile and potentially harmful addictions. Little wonder then that our social and health problems are on the rise. People have enough trouble controlling the sex drive without others fostering it on the young and thus prematurely increasing the intensity of the impulse far too early in life, especially during the maturation period.

During my own research I discovered that over the past few decades most medical doctors condone masturbation without reservation. Not a single word is mentioned about sublimation in the books written by these doctors (about 95% of "scientific" authors are in favor of masturbation). They are not aware that many people have the opposite view and have lived more productive lives as a result. Scientists are not infallible, and daily we read about complete reversals of their long-standing views. The case involving Louis Pasteur is a classic example. His *germ theory* of disease was unknown at the time, and he was met with much opposition from his colleagues. They were to be proved wrong. Later, Pasteur found a friend in Joseph Lister who was influenced by his work. That led to the use of antiseptics for the treatment of wounds.

One author, Dr. Donald Donohugh, seems to be opposed to masturbation in some instances:

> Masturbation was almost universally condemned until recent years. The last decade or two has [during the sexual revolution] seen a swing of opinion in favor of masturbation without further thought. But in masturbation, there is a certain denial of part of the person and his potential. It is a very lonely sex indeed, and for the most part, one seeks it only as a relief of tension. . . . It tends

toward the immoral if one's potential for socializing is shortcircuited by the more readily available sexual release of masturbation.[24]

Pornography, of course, is of equal importance and one of the most controversial topics in recent years. Worldwide, pornography has been both defended and vigorously opposed. One side claims the right to produce and sell whatever they choose if there is a demand, and the other side maintains that if it is not in the best interest of the public and the nation, if it is without redeeming social value, it should be restricted or banned. Should there be a limit? Where should the line be drawn? Many very concerned citizens emphatically say there should be a limit.

In a most timely book, Victor B. Cline, commented on the *Summary of the Report of the National Commission on Obscenity and Pornography.*

When questioned as to whether they favored access by adults or young persons to sexually explicit materials, about 40% of all respondents [in the survey conducted by the commission] made their response contingent on the issue of whether or not such material causes harm. About two-thirds of the persons who favor no legal restrictions said their views would change if it were clearly demonstrated that certain sexual materials have no harmful effects.[25]

It is apparent that many people are unable to determine what has a potential for harm and what does not. This raises the question of their educational level and whether or not they have studied published reports pertaining to the negative effects of pornography. It seems that not too many have studied these reports. The National Commission's Report is invaluable, notwithstanding the unreliable statistics from Denmark, which has a totally different culture and racial mix. In a certain sense, the report is flawed and misleading. However, it was acknowledged that not all cases of sexual crimes are reported, either in Denmark or in our own country. Thus, it is very difficult to accurately determine the value of the findings on the basis of such incomplete statistics.

Concluding his comments about the Commission's Report, Cline said:

> What this all suggested, in sum, is that the law is what we want it to be. Society shapes its laws more than the law or our constitution shapes society. And thus we permit as much freedom of expression and dramatic license as we wish. There is, however, probably somewhere a cost-benefit ratio. If speech becomes too disruptive and society suffers too much, in our self-interest we say "no"; we draw the line; we refuse to tolerate it. However, it takes some kind of sizeable consensus of our citizenry to draw the line. . . .[26]

He makes it clear that it will take a majority of citizens to win over a vociferous minority which is the main source of disruption and suffering. Fortunately, many are joining the battle against those forces.

Various studies have noted the damaging effects

of widespread perverse forms of behavior including "group sex."

Some very skilled attorneys protect and defend pornographers by using every loophole in the law, misinterpreting the constitution, and hiding behind "freedom of speech and freedom of press." In most cases they succeed due to public apathy, laxity of the laws, and sympathetic judges who are a part of the problem. Those who continue to purchase pornographic works are also accessories to the crimes.

Perhaps the most damaging evidence against pornography was the commission-sponsored study "Sex Offenders Report Pornography as a Contributor to Their Crimes":

That the sex offenders significantly more often than their controls [nonsex offenders with whom they were compared] increased their sexual activity after viewing pornography. A significant minority (39%) of the sex offenders indicated that "pornography had something to do with their committing the sex offense they were convicted of." The researchers also found that their offenders significantly more often claimed they had been influenced by pornography to commit a sexual crime.[27]

An expert "witness" testified:

Pornography teaches a degraded view of human beings, depriving them of their specifically human character. Sexual activity normally takes place as a part of a personal relationship between two people, not as a mere physical act. But "when sex is public, the viewer does not see—cannot see—the sentiments and the ideals. He can only see the

71

animal coupling. . . . When sex is a public spectacle, a human relationship has been debased into a mere animal connection." To learn that one relationship is merely animal, is to learn something which is likely to carry over into other relationships.

Pornography "appeals to and provokes a kind of sexual regression," "a return to infantile sexuality." "Put bluntly, it is a masturbatory exercise of the imagination." This too impairs the ability for healthy adult relationships, and by extension the ability to maintain the responsible creative kind of interrelationship which is human civilization.[28]

Indeed, pornography is a menace to our society and the sooner we are able to outlaw it and prosecute the offenders, the better it will be for our country. It breeds criminality. Boris Sokoloff states:

Nations in the stage of decline and disintegration such as Ancient Egypt or the Roman Empire, were particularly involved in the extremities of sexual relations. But now it appears that we were wrong in our belief that nothing new can be offered to demoralize human beings. New horizons in the field of sex are proclaimed by young American radicals.[29]

Several pages which followed gave an account of the activity of a former assistant professor of sociology at one of the Eastern universities. He had started a new movement dedicated to total sexual freedom and nudity, and from his plush westside apartment in Manhattan, recruited members of his anti-establishment society. He claimed "the source of man's unhappiness lies in the repression of sex."

If an assistant professor is of that caliber, how many more might be just as irrational? How many students had he corrupted before he became an ex-associate professor?

Another more disturbing and reprehensible case was noted in the AP Report (August 19, 1989): "An associate college professor who was fired after he admitted exposing himself to two female colleagues . . . at the urban studies department. He won an appeal for reinstatement and "the university officials will allow his return to the classroom when classes resume September 5."

The previous two cases are examples of what has been going on in some of our institutions of higher learning. It tells us of the threat to our society by unethical professors. It signifies the perils confronting us and how much has to be done to help reverse the trend toward total decay. We have had enough warnings.

Further research efforts revealed that many authors, including several doctors, are advocating that sexual activities be continued well past the middle years—among those who can least afford the luxury of erotic activities. Such suggestions are quite common at present, and the claim is that there is no significant danger or ill effects. This view differs from those of some great philosophers and other prominent writers.

In his old age, the great Greek dramatist, Sophocles (496–406) was asked,

> How are you on sex? Can you still have intercourse with a woman? He said, 'Most joyfully did I escape it, as though I had run away from a sort of frenzied and savage master.'[30]

Plato added these comments:

> I thought at that time, he had spoken well and I still do, for in every way, old age brings peace and freedom from such things [among those who have learned to discipline themselves well]. When the [sexual] desires cease to strain and finally relax, then what Sophocles says comes to pass in every way; it is possible to be rid of very many mad masters. . . . There is one cause, not old age, Socrates, but the character of human beings.

It is evident in modern times that many fully understand what Sophocles and Plato were saying. They have profited by sublimation and sexual self-disciplining. The findings of these philosophers have motivated those who have studied their works to adopt their principles and thereby enrich their lives. Complete mastery over the sex-drive is possible. (It might surprise some people to know that "sexual impotency" is welcomed by many.)

By virtue of sublimation and a well-ordered sex life, moderation was their policy. Some of the healthy elderly have become volunteer workers in many fields of community services—aged citizens have been and are working in the "peace corps," helping others less fortunate throughout the world.[31]

It is apparent that the more one has cultivated various interests apart from the erotic—hobbies, reading of constructive literature, music, art, sports, history, religion, philosophy, sociology—the more capable one is of controlling the sexual impulse and diverting sexual energies to other channels. A person who has not cultivated other interests is at risk of becoming enslaved by sexual addiction.

Some people become actively involved in worthy community or church activities. This is especially true of senior citizens who no longer feel it is necessary to continue an active sex life. They derive much joy in giving of themselves—in helping the less fortunate.

The other extreme, the libertines and sexual addicts, devote no time to community activities. They contribute nothing of real value to our society and are the ones who create most of our social problems. Many of them are beyond reason; they cannot understand the harm they are doing to themselves and the reduction of their potential. *This lost generation may never be reached;* we may not be able to help them overcome their self-inflicted handicaps. But we must continue to try to help those who can still be helped. The younger generations can profit from the mistakes of their elders.

It is apparent that wife-beating and abuse quite often results when the husband has been dehumanized by his insatiable sexual appetite. This is why it is so important to understand the principles involved in the philosophy and psychology of sex described here and in the works of others who are equally concerned about our related social problems.

Another author expressed some pertinent views on this vital subject:

> The person whose past experience with sex has been that of the hungry animal, or that of the egotistic philanderer who has thought of his partner essentially as [a sex object merely and] a means for his enjoyment, will not have an easy time meeting a new situation in which his highest nature wants expression for the sake of his beloved. From the point of view of married life as a whole, the person who has learned to think of human beings as "males" or "females" who can be "used" may indeed find and create more trouble than he can imagine.

> It would be tragic to underemphasize the importance of such psychological influences.[32]

The Sexual Addict

What is a sexual addict? How does he become addicted? First and foremost, a sexual addict is one who is almost always preoccupied with sexual fantasies and the subsequent involvement in erotic activities. Nothing is too base or perverted for him to engage in as long as it satisfies his ravenous sexual appetite.

The semi-addict does not go as far, but also indulges excessively in erotic activities, either through masturbation or with any willing partner or a prostitute. Most often both kinds of sexual addicts are obsessed with pornography which no doubt contributes to their sexual addiction. Some become addicted without the "aid" of pornography—through their ignorance of the adverse effects of overindulgence or influences in their particular culture or sub-culture. There are several factors involved in these dehumanizing activities.

Films, plays, and pornographic literature, are among the chief contributing factors which produce sexual addicts. Many motivated by greed, deny the adverse effects of their "business." And in fostering sexual promiscuity they help spread AIDS.

One answer to this problem is to boycott their productions *and* their sponsors.

Proper sex education in all of our schools is one of the best means of prevention of sexually delinquent behavior, and prevention is far less costly than curing—and in some extreme cases there is no cure. Some delinquents become rapists and even sexually abused children result. Some become incorrigible and contribute to the delinquency of others; many become unfit parents in their teens.

Sex gluttony, like food gluttony, tends to destroy the individuals who persist in *overindulgence*. In either case, the addicts pay the penalty—what they found to be most joyful, ultimately becomes painful and detrimental. They never learned the value of moderation and sublimation.

INCEST

The increase in this most alarming, reprehensible,

and dehumanizing form of human sexual behavior during the sexual revolution was recently discussed on the *Geraldo TV Program*. The therapist for incest victims, Dr. Charles Citrenbaum, said:

> Incest is the most horrendous, horrible thing I've confronted. . . . It is very prevalent, Geraldo. It's more than a few hundred thousand people; it's in the millions. Some pretty good research says that one out of every four or five females have been at least molested or inappropriately touched, and one out of every seven or eight males. We're talking about millions of people. It is a conservative [estimate].[33]

It is evident how much trauma and emotional harm is wrought by such behavior which results in the need for therapy in almost all cases. There is no estimate of the number of unreported cases of incest, but that number could be much greater than has been reported. Such sexual perverts are not always caught and prosecuted. We cannot afford to allow such conditions to exist and to increase. It appears that unscrupulous step-parents are the worst offenders and many natural fathers. In recent years we have read other such alarming reports.

Notes

1. Norman Vincent Peale, *Sin, Sex, and Self-Control*. Doubleday & Co., Inc., Garden City New York, 1965, p. 48
2. Ibid.
3. CLF (Formerly CDL) Reporter, Vol. 26, No. 6, July–August

1989, 2845 E. Camelback Road, Suite 740, Phoenix, Arizona 85016.

4. Allan Bloom, *The Republic of Plato* (The Collected Dialogues), Basic Books, 1968, 1404–1405.

5. Steven M. Cahn, *Classics of Western Philosophy* (Aristotle's Nicomachean Ethics), Hacket Publishing Company, Indianapolis, Indiana, 1977, p. 162.

6. Frierich Paulsen, *A System of Ethics*, Charles Scribner's Sons, New York, 1899, pp. 268, 343.

7. Boris Sokoloff, *The Permissive Society*, Arlington House, New Rochelle, N.Y., 1971, pp. 5, 7.

8. Ibid., pp. 181–207.

9. E. H. Staffelback, *Moral Crisis in America*, Pageant Press, New York, 1964, pp. 33, 15.

10. George Charles Roche III, *The Bewildered Society*, Arlington House, New Rochelle, New York, 1972, p. 327.

11. Max Rafferty, *What They Are Doing to Our Children*, New American Library, 1963, pp. 49–50.

12. Alexis Carrel, *Man the Unknown*, Halcyon House, New York, 1938, p. 143.

13. Napoleon Hill, *Think and Grow Rich*, Wilshire Book Company, North Hollywood, CA, 1966, pp. 220, 218.

14. Gabrielle Brown, *The New Celibacy*, McGraw-Hill, New York, 1980.

15. Wardell B. Pomeroy, *Boys and Sex and Girls and Sex,* Delacorte Press, New York, 1981, Chapters 3, 4, 5, 6, 7.

16. Winifred V. Richmond, *Hygiene of Personality*, Farrar and Rinehart, New York, 1936, p. 173.

17. Karl Menninger, *Whatever Became of Sin,* Hawthorne Books, New York, 1973, p. 140.

18. Herbert Benson, *The Relaxation Response*, William Morrow and Company, New York, 1975, p. 56.

19. *Readings in Psychology* (1977–1978) Annual Editions, p. 60, Dushkin Publishing Group, Inc., Sluice Dock, Guilford, Connecticut.

20. Ibid., p. 61.

21. Ibid., p. 63, 64.
22. Leopold Bellak and Harvey H. Barten, *A Progress in Community Mental Health,* Brunner/Mazel Publishers, New York, 1975, pp. 271–315.
23. Ibid., pp. 274–275.
24. Donald L. Donohugh, *The Middle Years* (A Physician's Guide to Your Body), Philadelphia, Pennsylvania, Saunders Press, 1981, pp. 140, 246–247.
25. Victor B. Cline (editor), *Where Do You Draw the Line,* Brigham Young University Press, Provo, Utah, 1974, pp. 181–182.
26. Ibid., p. 199.
27. Ibid., p. 107.
28. Ibid., p. 226.
29. Boris Sokoloff, *The Permissive Society,* Arlington House, New Rochelle, NY, 1971, pp. 181–182.
30. Allan Bloom, *The Republic of Plato, Basic Books Inc.,* 1968. p. 5, C. Antonio Provost, *The Sexual Revolution: Its Impact on Society.* . . . Vantage Press, Inc. New York, 1985, pp. 23–24.
31. Richard Wasserstrom, *Today's Moral Problems,* "The Human Venture in Sex, Love and Marriage" by Peter A. Bertocci on "Sexual Morality," Macmillan Company, Inc., New York, N.Y., 1975, pp. 223–224.
32. *Senior Volunteers in the Peace Corps,* Peace Corps, p. 301, Washington, D.C. 20526 (free literature).
33. *Transcripts: Journal Graphics Inc.,* "Incest Survivors Fight Back," August 23, 1989, transcript #505, New York, NY.

Chapter VI

CONCLUSION

The opportunity to make this a far better nation and to advance humanity is at hand. What each of us has witnessed personally and read about—the steady decline in morals, especially in our own country, the rise in crime, the broken homes, the abandoned and abused children, and a host of other disturbing problems—should provide sufficient motivation for a united effort to bring about the necessary reforms.

As more people become fully cognizant of the nature and extent of the problems, those who become involved in working for solutions will help change the attitudes of the indifferent and apathetic so that they, too, will contribute to the common good of society.

It is quite obvious it will be a very long struggle due to the present climate and the prevailing negative attitudes of most people. But there is much encouragement in the fact that many people— including writers and teachers have devoted much of their lives to the effort. Some of our university professors have made outstanding contributions over the past few decades. While there are shortcomings and defects in our schools of higher education as well as in secondary schools, some are very good; but even among those there is room for improvement.

It is true that much has been left unsaid here, and that greater research and documentation is required in order to address these enormously great and complex problems. But the start had to be made so that some immediate steps can be taken. Every moment of delay serves to compound the problems.

Indeed, this is an emergency, not only a national one, but universal because as America goes so goes the world. We have a leadership role, and we must show the world that we can produce citizens who are more humane and productive. We need to demonstrate this to the weaker and far less educated and prosperous nations. If we are weak morally, spiritually, and physically, we cannot be genuine leaders.

I appeal to our national and local leaders to seriously consider the issues raised here and institute legislation that will help solve the problems. Most books referred to here are available to all for reference. However, I quote the judicious remarks of Leon Gutterman, the editor and publisher of *Wisdom* (long out of print).

Great books are the key to man's culture. If they vanished overnight and could not be replaced, our civilization would disappear [to a certain extent, in a certain sense].

Great books are a treasure, a precious storehouse. They contain enough to make us rich for time and eternity. They contain the secret for happy living. They contain the key of wisdom.[1]

It has been written: "The regime of philosopher-kings is usually ridiculed and regarded as totalitarian, but it contains much of what we really want. Practically everyone wants reason to rule. . . ."[2]

It is sad indeed that "An American high school student knows only the word 'philosophy' and it does not appear to be any more serious a life choice than yoga."[3] This professor-philosopher's remark sums up in a few words the vacuum that exists in our schools.

The all-important works and philosophy and the many findings of authors who are in the sociological field, were vital elements. It is largely the motivation and the inspiration engendered by them that I became involved in this kind of activity in order to be of service to our country and humanity.

While the subject of pornography has been dealt with, a few more points should be made. The editor of *Plain Truth*,[4] Joseph W. Tkach, concluded:

Pornography isn't what it used to be! Modern modes of filming, printing, electronic reproductions and telecommunications have changed all that. . . .

83

By the late 1960s, a new breed of sexually oriented books and films came into the market. Restraints upon language and descriptions of sexual activities were gradually eliminated. But the proliferation of photographically explicit sexual materials—usually termed hard-core-pornography—took place in the '70s. At first simulated sexual acts were shown. Soon closeups of real acts were depicted.

What all this adds up to is quite obvious:

Pornography creates perverse sexual addictions. Victor Cline, clinical psychologist and professor of psychology at the University of Utah and an expert on pornography, has found addiction to pornography among hundreds of users of pornography he has worked with. . . .

Pornography is a strong measure of the decadence of the individual, a community or a nation [when it is a widespread industry and purchased and used by a large percent of the population].

The article goes on to tell of the "humiliation of women" which ". . . is centered in pornography. Women are to be used and then discarded." He records its impact on the family and society as a whole:

If you are a parent, set the right example in your values and behavior by what you read, watch and say. Teach children wholesome and responsible attitudes toward sex and other persons by how you talk to and treat other persons. Make plain the evils of pornography and sex abuse.

There can be no better advice than that on the subject.

In view of the harm being done by the pornographers and their industry, are they not traitors? They disseminate their poisonous wares at the expense of our people and our nation. No foreign enemies have been able to do as much damage as our enemies within. Their accomplices are those who purchase their merchandise including the "highly educated," who are totally unaware that they are a part of the problem. It is apparent that *early in a student's life, proper education* on the adverse effects of pornography is one of the best remedies.

If the adult accomplices to these crimes are too far gone to change their attitudes, then let us devote our energies to the young.

In Denmark, the sale and distribution of pornography has been legalized, and there are no statistics to prove it is harmful to the individual or causes sexually related crimes. If this is so, perhaps it is because they have the kind of education which counteracts the effects and dissuades their population from purchasing the pornographic materials which are exported to our country and others.

This conjecture may be fortified by the following information:

Religion and Education. Almost all Danes are Lutherans, and the Evangelical Lutheran Church is the established church of Denmark. About 100,000 persons profess other faiths, the majority of these being Roman Catholic. The entire population of Denmark is literate. Education is compulsory for all from the age of seven to fourteen, and, for the most part, free.[5]

In the U.S. religion is not an integral part of our public education; we have no "established church"; we have total separation of church and state.

And, of course, we do not know the actual effect of the legalization of the sale and distribution of pornographic material. Pornography was not always acceptable there or legalized in Denmark. As mentioned before, it has steadily increased in our country within the past two decades, and we *do* know the effect it has had on us.

The dominance of religion in Denmark and its presence in the school system, along with the 100% literacy rate, are factors to be considered. Without these factors in the U.S., pornography can be far more attractive. Seduction is much easier.

An illiterate person, for the most part, is almost impossible to teach the harm that is done by pornography. And the pornographers know how to exploit the gullible and illiterate. It also can be concluded that our high rate of illiteracy is partly due to the side-effects of pornography. A mind poisoned by these products loses the capacity to think rationally. Even the semi-illiterate are vulnerable because of the ease with which visual materials such as photos, films, and videos are obtained and viewed.

A brief admonishment by the author and social anthropologist, J. D. Unwin, is appropriate here:

> Any human society is free to choose either to display great energy or to enjoy sexual freedom; the evidence is that it cannot do both for more than one generation. If continence

is great, the energy will be great: if the continence is small [and the potential energy is squandered on a very large scale], the energy will be small.[6]

The findings on sublimation or the *conversion of sexual energy* are worth considering. Although the correlation is not entirely clear, it appears that biochemistry holds the key to the unraveling of the phenomenon.[7] How this theorized conversion occurs is a matter which requires much more study.

What appears to have specific relevancy to sublimation and the conservation and/or conversion of sexual energy is in the following findings:

The demonstration of the laws of conservation of matter and energy has been made again and again for animate as well as inanimate matter. Matter is transformed chemically and physically, but none is lost and none gained; energy is changed from one form to another, but here too, is neither lost nor gained.[8]

It is not certain how much this might apply to the theory of sublimation, but it provides a sound basis for further study.

Tho author goes on to say:

The interaction of the glands of internal secretion has been noted in several connections. . . . Undoubtedly many other relationships [have been discovered].[9]

Since the sex glands are internal secretion organs, it can be safely assumed that the above is applicable. Thus, the prolonged and unnecessary squandering of sexual secretions would be a negative factor. There would be less to conserve and/or convert in the process of sublimation.

The author was addressing the topic of metabolism (the process by which a substance is handled in the body, or the process of building up or breaking down the substance of plants or animals incidental to life), and there appears to be a correlation between sublimation and the conversion of sexual energy and the process involved in orgasms.

What conclusion can be drawn from this and other evidence previously cited? It is evident that if a person becomes a sex addict—persists in excessive sexual activities, his or her potential will be reduced as a result. Collectively, our society will suffer; there will be lessened productivity and creativity in direct relation to the number of people involved and the degree of sexual activities.

Further reference to biochemistry may shed more light on the subject of *sublimation*.

Biochemical Energetics provide some pertinent data:

> The concept of useful energy has been of great value in biochemistry because oxidation reactions in the cell are viewed as liberating energy that the cell can utilize for its vital functions, be it muscle contractions, the transmission of nerve impulse, or the synthesis of nucleic acids or proteins. Chemical thermodynamics deals with the energy relationships among chemical reactions. . . . Thermodynamics, or energetics, considers the rules that govern

the transition of a material system (such as chemical reaction from one state to another). Classical thermodynamics is completely independent of any concept of molecular structure, but rather concerns itself with the behavior of systems based on facts relating to energy changes from one state to another.[10]

It appears that the "sexual system" can and does undergo a change of energy "from one state to another," apart from its origin. The question of whether or not the theory is completely validated may not be answered for many more years of research.

Some people, through their experiences over a period of days or years, have discovered that too much sexual activity has deleterious effects. If they are intellectually honest, they will readily admit that there is direct evidence in support of this finding. Those who have changed a lifestyle of inordinate sexual activities to one of greater abstinence have so stated.[11]

A statement found in *Kybernetics* is appropriate to this discussion:

> You have often heard the expressions "sublimation of the libido" in reference to artistic creation. Libido is the Latin for lust, and sublimation of libido refers to the diversion of lust or sexual impulses from creation on a bodily plane to creation on a mental level. . . .[12]

A recent book on *Biochemistry* specifically notes the value of sperm:

The most compacted DNA is found in sperm heads in which histones are replaced by protomines, a series of . . . rich proteins. . . .[13]

The first law of thermodynamics states that the total energy of a system and its surroundings is a constant. In other words, energy is conserved.[14]

Human seminal plasma is a mixture of a variety of glands and tubular epithelial linings. . . . The analysis of proteins are most discordant, both qualitatively and quantitatively, but most of the work by electroporetic methods indicates that the protein fractions [in seminal plasma] are qualitatively identical with those of the blood serum.[15]

From such scientific information, it is apparent that biochemical components, originally of a sexual nature, have potential energy.

All over America there are smart, even gifted people who have a built-in passion for science. But that passion is unrequited. A recent survey suggested that 95% of Americans are "scientifically illiterate."[16]

It is evident that we are *a nation at risk*. What must be done to avoid the total destruction of our country has been clearly delineated.

The Stoic Philosopher, Marcus Aurelius, stated:

Consequently, if possible, as every impression of argument presents itself, consider its real nature and proper qualities, and reason with yourself about it. . . . Remember that to change your opinion and to follow him who corrects your error is not a surrender of freedom. Your action follows your own judgment and understanding and keeps the course your mind has set.[17]

With regard to the subject of human sexual behavior, our nation appears to be akin to St. Augustine's "City of God"—a city of "false, wicked and proud gods, who, because they are deprived of that unchangeable light which was meant for all, are reduced to a pitiful power, and therefore are eager for some sort of influence and demand divine honors from their deluded subjects."[18] It is clearly evident that two such forces exist within our country and the rest of the world.

The following statement by the Scottish philosopher, John Stewart Mill (1806–1873), supports what educators and sociologists have concluded pertaining to the environmental impact on the formation of one's character and mode of behavior:

If we knew the person thoroughly and knew all the inducements which are acting upon him, we could foretell his conduct with as much certainty as we can predict any physical event [after knowing the causes before it happened.][19]

Sociologists, psychologists and psychiatrists refer to "the social loop" and "interface"[20]—the place at which two independent systems meet and act on or communicate with each other. By such knowledge, sociological phenomena can be understood and explained satisfactorily. The interaction of systems and their sociological and psychological impact is evident in many cases. We need to know of the latest development in the field of psychology and other disciplines to be successful in understanding the interaction which occurs and how best to solve some of our major social problems.

Notes

1. Leon Gutterman, editor and publisher (Reprint of the original edition of Wisdom Magazine), *Wisdom of the Great Books of the Western World,* Beverly Hills, California, 1960, p. 1.
2. Allan Bloom, *The Closing of the American Mind,* Simon and Schuster, NY, 1987, p. 267.
3. Ibid., p. 377.
4. *Plain Truth* (Editor, Joseph W. Tkach), Worldwide Church of God, Pasadena, California, pp. 20–22.
5. *Funk & Wagnalls, Standard Reference Encyclopedia,* Vol. 8, 1964, p. 2696.
6. J. D. Unwin, *Sex and Culture,* Oxford University Press, London, England, 1933.
7. James M. Orten and Otto W. Neuhaus, *Biochemistry* (8th Edition), C. V. Mosby Company, St. Louis, Missouri, 1970, pp. 512, 505–506, 580–588, 666.
8. Ibid., p. 512.
9. Ibid., p. 505.
10. Benjamin H. Harrow and Abraham Mazur, *Text Book of Biochemistry,* 4th edition, W. B. Saunders Company, Philadelphia, PA, 1966, p. 81.
11. Gabrielle Brown, *The New Celibacy,* McGraw-Hill, 1980.
12. Stanley Jones, *Kybernetics of Mind and Brain,* Charles Mannerstone House, Springfield, IL, 1970, p. 158.

13. Lubert Stryer, *Biochemistry,* 3rd edition, W. H. Freeman & Company, New York, 1988, p. 830.
14. Ibid., p. 180.
15. James M. Orten and Otto W. Neuhaus, *Biochemistry* (8th edition), C. V. Mosby Company, St. Louis, MO, 1970, p. 666.
16. Carl Sagan, *Parade Magazine,* "Why We Need to Understand Science," New York, NY, September 10, 1989, p. 6.
17. Classic Club, *Marcus Aurelius and His Times,* Walter J. Black, Inc. Roslyn, NY, 1945, p. 82.
18. St. Augustine, *The City of God* (edited by Vernon J. Bourke), Image Books, Doubleday & Company Division, Garden City, NY, 1950, pp. 204–205.
19. F. Gene Acuff, *From Man to Sociology,* The Dryden Press, Hinsdale, Ill., 1973, p. 56.
20. Lorant Forizs, *Loops and Interfaces of Man,* Libra Publishers, San Diego, CA., 1977.

BIBLIOGRAPHY

Acuff, Gene F., *From Man to Society,* the Dryden Press, Hinsdale, IL, 1973.

Adler, Mortimer, *Aristotle for Everybody,* Bantam Books, New York, 1978.

Albert, Ethel, Theodore C. Denise and Sheldon P. Peterfreund, *Great Traditions and Ethics,* D. Van Nostrand Company, New York, 1975.

Alexander, Dan, Jr., *Who is Ruining Our Schools,* Research Education *Foundation,* Washington, D.C., 1986.

Augustine, St., *The City of God* (Edited by Vernon J. Bourke), Image Books, Doubleday & Company, Garden City, New York, 1950, pp. 204–205.

Berger, Peter, *Invitation to Sociology,* Anchor Books, Doubleday & Company, Inc., New York, 1963.

Bambrough, Renford, *The Philosophy of Aristotle,* New American Library, New York, 1962.

Benet, Sula, "Why They Live to Be 100 or Even Older in Abkhasia," *Focus Aging,* Dushkin Publishing Company, Guilford, Connecticut, 1978.

Bennett, Thomas Peter, and Earl Frieden, *Modern Topics in Biochemistry,* MacMillan Co., 1967.

Benson, Herbert, *The Relaxation Response,* William Morrow & Company, 1975.

Bloom, Allan, *The Republic of Plato,* Basic Books, New York, 1968.

Bloom, Allan, *The Closing of the American Mind,* Simon and Schuster, New York, 1987.

Brecher, Edward M., and Jeremy, *Human Sexuality,* Dushkin Publishing Group, Guilford, Connecticut, 1979–1980.

Brown, Barbara, *Readings in Psychology,* "Biofeedback. . . ." Dushkin Publishing Group, Ibid., 1980.

Brown, Gabrielle, *The New Celibacy,* McGraw-Hill, New York, 1980.

Bryson, Lyman, *An Outline of Man's Knowledge of the Modern World*, Nelson Doubleday, Garden City, New York, 1960.

Cahn, Steven M., *Classics of Western Philosophy*, "Aristotle's Nicomachean Ethics," Hackett Publishing Company, 1977.

Carrel, Alexis, *Man the Unknown*, Halcyon House, New York, 1938.

CLF Reporter (formerly CDL, Citizens for Decent Literature), Phoenix, Arizona, July/August, 1989, Vol. 26, No. 6.

Cheney, Lynne V., *National Endowment for the Humanities*, "A Core Curriculum for College Students," Washington, D.C., Nov./Dec. 1989.

Christenson, Cornelia V., *Kinsey, A Biography*, Indiana University Press, Bloomington, Indiana, 1971.

Classic Club, *Marcus Aurelius and His Times*, Walter J. Black, Inc. Roslyn, New York, 1945, p. 62.

Cline, Victor B., *Where Do You Draw the Line?*, Brigham University Press, Provo, Utah, 1974.

Davis, Philip E., *Dialogues of Modern Philosophy*, Allyn and Bacon, Boston, 1977.

Donohugh, *The Middle Years*, The Saunders Press, Philadelphia, Pennsylvania, 1981.

Evans, Bergen, *Dictionary of Quotations*, Delacorte Press, New York, 1968.

Full, Harold, *Controversy in American Education*, MacMillan Company, New York, 1967.

Forizs, Lorant, *Loops and Interfaces of Man*, Libra Publishers, San Diego, CA, 1977.

Gordon, Michael, *Old Enough to Feel Better (A Medical Guide for Seniors)*, Radnor, Pennsylvania, Chilton Book Company, 1981.

Graham, Billy, *The World Aflame*, Doubleday & Company, Inc., New York, 1965.

Grisex, Germain and Russell Shaw, *The New Morality*, University of Notre Dame Press, South Bend, Indiana, 1974.

Gutterman, Leon (editor/publisher), *Wisdom of the Great Books of the Western World*, Beverly Hills, California, 1960.

Hamilton, Edith and Huntington Cairns, *Plato, Collected Dialogues,* Princeton University Press, Princeton, New Jersey, 1961.

Harrow, Benjamin and Abraham Mazur, *Text Book of Biochemistry,* 4th edition, W. B. Saunders Company, Philadelphia, Pennsylvania, 1966.

Harper, H. A. and W. W. Rodwell, P. A. Mayes, et. al., *Review of Physiological Chemistry,* 7th Edition, Lange Medical Publications, Los Altos, California, 1979.

Harrity, Richard and Ralph G. Martin, *The Three Lives of Helen Keller,* Doubleday, Garden City, NY, 1963.

Hill, Napoleon, *Think and Grow Rich,* Wilshire Book Company, North Hollywood, California, 1966.

Hite, Shere, *The Hite Report,* MacMillan Company, New York, 1976.

Holt, Rackham, *George Washington Carver,* Doubleday & Company, Garden City, New York, 1943.

Jacquet, Lou, "Juvenile sex offenders: Distressingly commonplace," *Our Sunday Visitor,* Huntington, In., June 25, 1989, p. 3.

Jones, Stanley, *Kybernetics of Mind and Brain,* Charles Bannerstone House, Springfield, Illinois, 1970.

Keller, James, *To Light A Candle, The Autobiography of James Keller,* Doubleday and Company, Garden City, New York, 1963.

Kinsey, Albert, et al., *Sexual Behavior in the Human Male,* W. B. Saunders Company, Philadelphia, Pennsylvania, 1948. *Sexual Behavior in the Human Female,* Ibid., 1943.

Labin, Suzanne, *Hippies, Drugs* and *Promiscuity,* Arlington House, New Rochelle, NY, 1972.

Link, Henry C., *The Return to Religion,* MacMillan Company, NY, 1936.

Loomis, Louise, Ropes, *Aristotle on Man in the Universe,* Classic Club, Walter L. Black, Roslyn, NY, 1943.

McMurray, Linda O., *George Washington Carver,* Oxford University Press, New York and Oxford, 1981.

McQuade, Walter and Ann Aikman, *The Longevity Factor*, Simon and Schuster, New York, 1979.

Martin, Rose L., *The Selling of America*, Fidelis Publishing Company, Santa Monica, California, 1973.

Menninger, Karl, *Whatever Became of Sin?*, Hawthorne Books, New York, 1973.

Millikan, Robert A., *The Autobiography of Robert A. Millikan*, Prentice-Hall, 1950.

Orten, James M. and Otto W. Neuhaus, *Biochemistry*, C. V. Mosby Company, St. Louis, Missouri, 1970.

Paulsen, Friedrich, *A System of Ethics*, Charles Scribners Sons, New York, 1899.

Peale, Norman Vincent, *Sin, Sex and Self Control*, Doubleday & Company, Garden City, NY, 1965.

Pikunas, Justin, *Human Development*, McGraw-Hill, NY, 1976.

Provost, C. Antonio, *The Sexual Revolution: Its Impact on Society. . . .* Vantage Press, New York, 1985.

The Birth of the Modern Renaissance, Pageant Press, New York, 1965.

Rafferty, Max, *What They Are Doing to Our Children*, New Amsterdam Library, New York, 1963.

Suffer Little Children, The Devin-Adair Company, New York, 1962.

Richmond, Winifred V., *Hygiene of Personality*, Farrar & Rinehart, New York, 1937.

Roche, George Charles, III, *The Bewildered Society*, Arlington House, New Rochelle, New York, 1972.

Saxon, Lloyd, *The Individual Marriage and the Family*, Wadsworth Publishing Company, Belmont, California, 1972.

Sokoloff, Boris, *The Permissive Society*, Arlington House, New York, 1971.

Sorokin, Pitrim, *Contemporary Sociological Theories*, Harper Brothers, New York, 1928.

Staffleback, E. H., *Moral Crisis in America*, Pageant Press, 1964.

Strekler, Bernard, *Gerontological Research,* Volume 4, Academic Press, New York, 1972.

Tkach, Joseph W., *Plane Truth,* "Pornography, Does it Really Hurt Anyone?" Worldwide Church of God, Pasadena, California, September, 1989.

Unwin, J. D., *Sex and Culture,* Oxford University Press, London, England, 1933.

Wallin, Paul, *American Sociological Review,* "An Appraisal of Some Methodological Aspects of the Kinsey Report," April, 1949.

Wasserman, Richard, *Today's Moral Problems,* MacMillan, NY, 1975.

ADDENDUM

... Men of genius, in addition to their powers of observation and comprehension, possess other qualities, such as intuition and creative imaginationn. Through intuition they learn things ignored by other men, they perceive relations between seemingly isolated phenomena. . . .

Dr. Alexis Carrel

It is important to include more recent pertinent information pertaining to the crime rate and the threat to our children. An AP August 7, 1989 report stated:

A record 20,675 Americans were murdered in 1988 for an increase of 2.9 percent over the previous year, the FBI says, while the number of aggravated assaults rose by 6.6 percent to 910,000.

The Uniform Crime Reports for 1988 said the number for all violent crimes—including rape and robbery increased—increased by 5.5 percent to a new high of 1.56 million. The previous high was 1.48 million in 1987.[1]

The report also noted that "The rate of crime per 100,000 people in 1988 rose 2.1 percent, and the violent crime rate increased 1.8 percent." There are no immediate signs that the crime rate in 1989 and 1990 will decrease. The hoped for reforms in education and change in the environment and social climate is not expected to take effect for quite a few more years.

99

In *"America's Children at Risk,"*[2] the author concluded:

> There is hope in the form of hundreds of thousands of dedicated individuals working to better the lives of children. And there is hope for the future—if the country acts now [before it is too late] to forestall the looming crisis. Says Phillip Porter, M.D., founder of Boston's Healthy Children program, "Early intervention is better than late intervention, but prevention is best of all."
>
> One route to prevention is public awareness. "We've got to make a critical mass of Americans understand that the breakdown of American family is a great threat," says Marian Edleman, president of the Children's Defense Fund.[3]

This excellent article describes the many problems facing our children and points out the urgent need for addressing them immediately. Some efforts being made toward the solution are presented, including the activities of senior citizens:

> Whether through advocacy efforts, political support or direct interventional programs (see "Reaching Across Generations" page 38), Older people can make a vast difference in the lives of America's children. When that happens everyone benefits: you, your children and grandchildren, and all future generations of Americans.[4]

Indeed! The older generation that has observed the decay of our country and the adverse influences on the younger generations can make a difference.

There are some encouraging signs of "the return to religion" this year, according to a *New York Times* news service report:[5]

After decades of shunning classroom discussion of religion, fearing it was too divisive a subject or that church-state separation might be breached, many American public schools are moving to incorporate it into their curricula.

The change results largely from a sentiment that schools have too long ignored religion as a force in American and world culture, and signs of it are far flung. . . .

Last August the Arizona Board of Education adopted an outline of "social studies essential skills" for its elementary and secondary schools that requires teaching the religious roots of ethical convictions and cultural differences.

Similarly, a year ago new guidelines from the California Department of Education informed school districts that "students must become familiar with the basic ideas of the major religions and ethical traditions of each time and place. . . ."

This most timely intervention is long overdue. The journalist concluded:

The coalition [working on the project for the National Council on Religion and Public Education] included the American Federation of Teachers, the National Association of Evangelicals, the Christian Legal Society, the National Council of Churches of Christians and Jews.

Alcohol, Drug Addiction and Religion

The national problem of drug addiction and the sale and distribution of harmful drugs needs to be addressed. *As in all other social problems, we must approach it by seeking out the root causes.* One answer to the problem may be found in the analysis of some of the methods used in the rehabilitation of drug and alcohol addicts. Knowing the underlying causes will provide methods for prevention.

It has been found that an element of religion is an important factor in the rehabilitation of addicts.

The following quotations provide evidence of its efficacy. Kathleen, a recovered alcoholic, said:

> There's a lot of spirituality in AA—go to a meeting and you can't help but pick it up. She believes this spirituality is important and that it works, even with a person like herself who is not very religious. She begins outlining the well known "twelve steps" of AA:

> Step 1, you admit you've become powerless over alcohol. In Step 2 you say that only a higher power can restore your sanity; in Step 3 you resolve to turn your life and will over to this higher power. In Step 4, you take moral inventory of yourself, and in Step 5, you share it with another person. . . .[6]

> Unquestionably, the most dramatic successes in coping with alcoholism belong to Alcoholics Anonymous. The effectiveness of this group is based on what amount to a conversion, a profound and quasi-religious phenomenon.[7]

It is apparent what that "higher power" is and how much of a religious experience is used in several other rehabilitation groups such as Synanon and Gamblers Anonymous.

Since these organizations have been successful in helping people recover from their addictions, it appears that including their methods in the high school curricula would be of value as a means of prevention as well as a cure for youngsters who are either on the path to addiction or are already addicted.

The following twelve steps appeared in a recent publication:

1. We admitted we were powerless over [problem], that our lives had become unmanagable.
2. We came to believe that a Power greater than ourselves could restore us to sanity.
3. We made a decision to turn our will and our lives over to the care of God as we understood Him.
4. We made a searching and fearless moral inventory of ourselves.
5. We admitted to God, ourselves, and to another human being the exact nature of our wrong.
6. We were entirely ready to have God remove all these defects of character.
7. We humbly asked God to remove our shortcomings.
8. We made a list of all persons we had harmed and became willing to make direct amends to them all.
9. We made direct amends to such people wherever possible, except when to do so would injure them or others.
10. We continued to take personal inventory and when we were wrong, promptly admitted it.
11. We sought through prayer and meditation to improve our conscious contact with God as we understood Him, praying only for knowledge of God's will for us, and the power to carry that out.

12. Having had a spiritual awakening as the result of these
    steps, we tried to carry this message to (others) and to prac-
    tice these principles in all our affairs.[8]

It is well known that some so-called religious people or church goers have become drug or alcohol addicts, but those who are devout in their particular
faith are never victimized by such destructive habits.

Fortunately, very few members of the clergy
have succumbed to alcoholism not because religion
failed them, but because they failed religion and
unjustly gave cause to discredit it.

Let's not judge religion by its imposters or worst
sinners, but by the faithful, the saints and those who
sincerely practice the faith they profess. Those who
defile their bodies and minds, "the temple of God,"
by their indiscretions such as drug or alcohol abuse
and claim to be religious, are deceiving themselves
and others as well. Tobacco addiction can be included
among these abuses.

But we must bear in mind that there are other
kinds of addictions that are constructive and can
help counteract those that are harmful. When a person becomes "addicted" to the pursuit of learning
and continues to study what is best for the preser-
vation of health and longevity, he will acquire the
knowledge to help him avoid all forms of harmful
addictions.

The latest report pertaining to pornography and
sex crimes indicates a worsening of the problem.
Under the headings: "The Consequences of Pornog-

raphy Are Too Extensive to Ignore" and "Laws: The Consumer of Obscenity Contributes to the Degradation of Individuals, Human Love and Society," the authors stated:

> Recently an indictment in Alexandria, Va. was brought to our attention. The charges involved a group of men who plotted to kidnap or purchase a young boy for the purpose of sexually molesting, torturing and then murdering him. The twist was that these men planned to film the whole ordeal for the sexual pleasure of other like-minded citizens—for profit. . . . Sadly, however, the consequences of hard-core and child pornography are too extensive to ignore. Their cost to individuals and to society is measured daily in our sexual-abuse rates. In America at least one in four women is sexually assaulted in her lifetime. Conservative estimates put the number of molested children at more than a million per year. . . .
>
> As a nation that prides itself on defending the rights of people everywhere, we need a collective determination to eliminate hard-core pornography. . . .
>
> We believe that just as all people need to stand up together to fight racial discrimination, illegal drugs and other social evils, so we must also stand together against illegal pornography.[9]

Many other people have raised their voices in opposition to this crippling sexual exploitation industry, but to no avail. It continues to dehumanize more and more people.

Ethical Absolutes vs. Relativism

The debate over absolutism and relativism has gone on for many decades and still rages in and out of academic circles. If our educators were to consider what the philosopher Emanual Kant (1724–1804) wrote about "The Moral Law"[10] and the hypothetical and the categorical imperatives, they would find much to convince most of them that there are valid grounds for the philosophy of ethical absolutes. In his chapter on "Fundamental Principles of the Metaphysic of Morals," Kant wrote:

> All imperatives [obligations] are expressed by the word *ought* [*or shall*], and thereby indicate the relation of an objective law of reason to a will which from its subjective constitution is not necessarily determined by it (an obligation). . . . That which is practically *good* however which determines that will by means of the conceptions of reason and consequently not from subjective causes, but objectively, that is, on principles which are valid for every rational being as such.[11]

More readily understandable is his definition of the imperatives.

> If now the action is good only as a means to *something else*, then the imperative is hypothetical; if it is conceived as good *in itself* and consequently as being necessarily the principle of a will which of itself conforms to reason, then it is *categorical*. . . .

> There is therefore but one categorical imperative, namely, this: *Act only on that maxim whereby thou canst at the same time will that it should be a universal law.* . . . Since the universality of the law according to which effects are produced constitutes what is properly called *nature* in the most general sense (as to form)—that is, the exist-

106

ence of things so far as determined by general law—the imperative of duty may be expressed thus: *Act as if the maxim of thy action were to become by thy will a universal law of nature.*

Kant gives a few examples to illustrate the principle of the categorical imperative:

We now enumerate a few duties, adopting the usual division of them into duties to ourselves and to others, and to perfect and imperfect duties.[12]

He concludes that suicide is not a duty or a categorical imperative.

A man reduced to despair by a series of misfortunes feels wearied of life, but is still so far in possession of his reason that he can ask himself whether it would not be contrary to his duty to himself to take his own life. . . . Now we see at once that a system of nature of which it would be a law to destroy life by means of the very feeling whose special nature it is to impel to the improvement of life would contradict itself, and therefore could not exist as a system of nature, hence that maxim cannot possibly exist as a universal law of nature, and consequently would be wholly inconsistent with the supreme principle of all duty.[13]

It is clearly evident that suicide when one is faced with painful experiences would not be good for society. It would be folly to condone it as an acceptable practice. Perhaps that is one reason why many people are against abortion or infanticide.

Another example of Kant's fundamental principle

of the metaphysic of morals and what should not be a "maxim for action" or a *universal law of nature* is the following:

> A third man finds in himself a talent which with the help of some culture might make him a useful man in many respects, but he finds himself in comfortable circumstances and prefers to indulge in pleasure rather than to take pains in enlarging and improving his natural gifts, besides agreeing with his inclinations to [over]indulge, agrees also with what is called duty. He sees then that a system of nature could indeed subsist with such a universal law, although men (like the South Sea Islanders) should let their talents rest and resolve to devote their lives merely to idleness, amusement, and propagation of their species—in a word to enjoyment; but he cannot possibly *will* that this should be a universal law of nature, or to be implanted in us as such by a natural instinct. . . .[14]

It is apparent that such a code of individual "morality," if universally adopted, would not be to the advantage of the human race. We have witnessed many people in our society whose "categorical imperatives" are just as Kant[15] described: It is morally wrong to waste talent and to dissipate when there is the opportunity to improve ourselves and to contribute significantly to society. This "imperative of duty" or obligation to one's self or to society is not promulgated by living under faulty principles.

Unfortunately, relativists such as the distinguished professor, Arthur Schlesinger Jr., assaults belief in "absolutes" and claims that relativism—in

108

religion, ethical life and politics—is what America is all about.[16]

It is apparent that *the main cause of our social and political* problems is the rejection of the philosophy based on absolutism and the prevalence of the doctrine of the relativists who do not believe there is a sound foundation for morality.

Virtue and Vice

The absolutists have determined what constitutes vice and what is virtue; the relativists are either not aware or stubbornly refuse to admit that the former is inherently an evil and the latter a good for humanity. Even when certain vices such as prostitution is legalized in some cities, states or countries, legalization does not make it less of a vice. The relativists, for the most part, condone what they believe does no harm to any person, being oblivious of the consequences of unethical sexual behavior. They believe that if there is a demand and the operation is well supervised and the victims examined regularly, it is acceptable.

They deny the mental and physical damage done to the prostitutes, even when proof is established. They believe that even if it is illegal, it is *only* a victimless crime. But the customers of this "oldest profession" are also victims, even though they may be unaware of the degradation and the risks involved.

Persons of virtuous character never participate in

109

any form of activities involving prostitution, and seldom if ever in sexual promiscuity or fornication.

Charity is another virtue worth considering—it is a charitable deed to promulgate (as so many philosophers have done) doctrines which explain the nature of vice and virtue. Genuine philosophers rarely make a profit through the works they undertake and publish. They do so for the love of humanity and the good of society. Those who do as philosophers have done are to be praised for their efforts.

A Final Defense of Philosophy
In defense of philosophers and philosophy, Plato had this to say:

> The world assumes that the philosopher's abstractions are folly, and rejects his guidance. The philosopher is the best kind of man; the corrupted philosopher is the worst; and the corrupting influence is irresistible to all but the very strongest natures |who are aware of their corruption and sophistry|. The professional teachers of philosophy live not by leading popular opinion |or the guidance toward the virtuous life| but by pandering to it; a bastard brood trick themselves out as philosophers while the true philosopher withdraws himself from so gross a world. Small wonder that philosophy gets discredited![17]

Indeed we have pseudo-philosophers—nihilists and hedonists—who have rejected the teachings of the world's great philosophers and substituted their own brand, much to the corruption of students and others.

110

The main mission of philosophy is:

> To make a genuine effort to understand other men's be-
> liefs and the reasons for them, provided that these beliefs
> are typical, earnest, and in basic harmony with the age,
> is an essential part of our attempt to know the world. A
> sympathetic knowledge of what others believe can only
> help us to make the choices we ourselves face. To be aware
> of others' solutions to ethical problems must eventually
> result in an increase in our own rational and thoughtful
> moral action.[18]

In Nagel's chapter on "The Mission of Philosophy,"
one learns the important role of philosophers
throughout the ages. The author concludes:

> ... The search for answers will, of course, inevitably go
> on. No matter how impressive our scientific knowledge
> may become, men will be restless until they can form a
> satisfactory picture of themselves in the kind of universe
> which science has revealed. The search will be a long,
> hard task, as long and hard as were those in the days
> when religion and philosophy provided a rationale for the
> evaluation of individual and social behavior. No task can
> be more vital to the welfare of mankind. The most urgent
> problem of the twentieth century is whether man today
> can discover and accept the demands which his conception
> of the universe puts upon him—the necessity to find his
> own place and society's place in the scheme of things be-
> fore he destroys himself by the abuse of the powers which
> science has given him.[19]

In Aristotle's *Nichomachean Ethics* he had much
to say about morality. In Chapter Two he stated:

111

Now if there is an end which has moral agents we seek for its own sake, and which is the cause of our seeking all the other ends—if we are not to go on choosing one act for the sake of another, thus landing ourselves in an infinite progression with the result that desire will be frustrated and ineffectual—it is clear that this must be the good, that is the absolute good. May we not then argue from this that knowledge of the good is a great advantage to us in the conduct of our lives? Are we not more likely to hit the mark if we have a target? If this be true |as I believe| we must do our best to get at least a rough idea of what the good really is, and which of the sciences, pure and applied, is concerned with the business of achieving it.[20]

What he wrote many centuries ago is important to consider at a time when the virtuous life is misunderstood and the life of vice is tolerated as never before in the history of humanity. Indeed, knowledge of the "absolute good" and knowledge of what constitutes the opposite when clearly illustrated will motivate more people to avoid behavior which is counterproductive and dangerous to society.

Aristotle's astute analytic delineation of the nature of genuine goodness and morality has enlightened millions of people who have studied his *Nicomachean Ethics,* a treatise dedicated to his son.

In the final analysis, do we not have to determine what is best for mankind before we can arrive at the means for its attainment?

One of the most encouraging recent developments in months is curriculum reform in higher education. In the 1989 November/December National Endowment for the Humanities publication, Chairman Lynne V. Cheney wrote:

> This report, *50 Hours,* is a way of informing colleges engaged in reform about how other schools are managing the task. Its aim is to be specific; its central device for organizing details is an imagined core of studies—fifty semester hours—that would encourage coherent and substantive learning in essential areas of knowledge.
>
> So far as I know, this particular core curriculum does not exist anywhere. Parts of it can be found at different colleges and universities; so can alternatives to both the parts and the whole.
>
> A required course of studies—a core of learning—can ensure that students have opportunities to know the literature, philosophy, institutions, and art of our own and other cultures.[21]

Mrs. Cheney, in reporting some reforms which have already begun in some colleges and universities said:

> The faculty of the remedial and developmental programs at Brooklyn College of the City of New York recently dedicated a conference to Brooklyn's core curriculum to recognize its importance for their work.
>
> In *50 Hours,* students are expected to write papers of varying length in every course, including those in science and mathematics [especially in philosophy].[22]

At Rice University in Houston where extensive curricular reform is under way, faculty members met in day-long sessions for two weeks last spring to discuss works to be taught in the humanities foundation course. A classicist

113

led discussion of the *Illiad*; a philosopher led discussion of Plato's *Republic*; a professor of music, of Mozart's *Marriage of Figaro.*[23]

In order to be better acquainted with this new program of reform devised by the National Endowment for the Humanities, a copy of *50 Hours, a Curriculum for College Students* will be sent free on request.*

(Perhaps Bloom's *The Closing of the American Mind* has been a kind of catalyst for getting educational reform started.) *The role of the National Endowment for the Humanities is a vital one for our nation; it is apparent that we are headed in the right direction. Could this be the beginning of the anticipated Modern Renaissance?*

Since a social problem is typically defined as a condition that must be corrected or improved to a tolerable level, an orderly and rational approach to a problem would demand an adequate description of the components of the problem, the sources of these, their mutual effects on each other, and the factors that might be introduced into the situation to eliminate or reduce the problem. . . . The scientific attack on a social problem may require the combined efforts of specialists from several unrelated |or related fields in order to achieve a lasting solution.|[24]

*Write to: Office of Publications and Public Affairs, National Endowment for the Humanities, 1100 Pennsylvania Avenue, N.W., Washington, D.C. 20506.

It seems fitting to conclude with this paragraph from the book, *Man The Unknown*:

For the first time in the history of humanity, a crumbling civilization is capable of discerning the causes of its decay. For the first time it has at its disposal the gigantic strength of science [as well as of genuine philosophy]. Will we utilize this knowledge and this power? It is our only hope of escaping the fate common to all great civilizations of the past. Our destiny is in our hands. On the new road, we must go forward.

Alexis Carrel

Notes

1. *The Los Angeles Times,* August 7, 1989, p. A2.
2. *Modern Maturity,* Lakewood, California, August–September 1989, p. 32.
3. Ibid., p. 35.
4. Ibid., p. 90.
5. *New York Times* Service, Peter Steinfels, April, 1989.
6. Walter McQuade and Ann Aikman, *The Longevity Factor,* Simon and Schuster, New York, 1979, pp. 140–141.
7. Joseph Julian, *Social Problems,* Appleton-Century-Crofts, Educational Division, Meredith Corporation, New York, 1973, p. 135.
8. John Catoir, *Christopher News Notes,* "Kicking the Habit," September 1989, New York.
9. Cardinal Joseph Bernardin and Rev. Eileen W. Lindner (a member of the Alliance Executive Committee, the National Council of Churches), "The Consequences of Pornography Are Too Extensive to Ignore," *The Los Angeles Times,* Nov. 12, 1989, p. M7.
10. Philip E. Davis, *Dialogues of Modern Philosophy,* Allyn and Bacon, Boston, MA, 1977, pp. 382–397.

11. Steven M. Cahn, *Classics of Western Philosophy,* Hackett Publishing Company, Indianapolis, IN, 1977, pp. 855–856.
12. Ibid., pp. 856–860.
13. Ibid., p. 860.
14. Ibid., p. 861.
15. Ibid., p. 860–861.
16. Michael Novak, *The National Catholic Register,* "Relativism or Absolutes: Which is the American Way," Studio City, CA, Oct. 1989, p. 5.
17. C. Antonio Provost, *The Sexual Revolution: Its Impact on Society,* Vantage Press, New York, 1985, pp. 89–90.
George Murray, "The Republic," *National Educational* Alliance, Inc., Vol. 2, Dunnellen, NJ, 1939, p. 104.
18. Lyman Bryson, *An Outline of Man's Knowledge of the Modern World,* Nelson Doubleday, Garden City, NY, 1960, p. 646.
19. Ibid., p. 677.
20. Steven M. Cahn, *Classics of Western Philosophy,* Hackett Publishing Company, Indianapolis, IN, 1977, pp. 115–116.
21. Lynne V. Cheney, "A Core Curriculum for College Students," National Endowment for the Humanities, November/December, 1989, p. 5.
22. Ibid., p. 7.
23. Ibid., p. 8.
24. F. Gene Acuff, Donald E. Allen and Lloyd A. Taylor, *From Man to Society,* The Dryden Press, Hinsdale, Illinois, 1973, p. 513.

(Author's poems from the *American Collegiate Poets,* fall 1976 and 1980, revised.)

An Ode to Alexander Pope

Now, we could use your sound philosophy—
So well composed in simple couplet rhymes,
You earned a name and fame in poets' history;
A man well suited to enlighten all,
One whose famous essays shed much light—
Today we still can profit from your splendid verse
To aid us set this troubled world aright and
End what to our progress is adverse.
You warned: "A little learning is a dangerous thing."
How few have understood just what you meant—
This decade your advice, reforms will bring
If foes and villains will at last relent;
Grateful are those who followed your advice
Acquiring wisdom born of your sacrifice.

An Ode to Plato

What sage has equalled his philosophy
Or his perceptiveness surpassed?
Within his dialogues so many centuries past,
How well did he expose the sophistry
Of blinded peers who led the blind astray
As those in modern times, from day to day.
Inspiring young and old alike to rise above
The common herd—to lead us to the proper paths
By virtue of his concepts near Divine,
The brilliance of his saintly soul
Enkindles our humanity
With sparks of spirituality.

How timely are the tenets of your *Laws* and
In *Republic's* principles!
If all could understand your messages
And the meaning of your lofty passages,
Your views could change this troubled world;
When your wisdom is unveiled—
There will be hope and less despair
But each of us must lend an ear.

An Ode to Aristotle (1989)

Aristotle, man for all the ages,
How could we so many years ignore your works,
Philosophy, sublime and logic so unique?
Though long ago you wrote to educate humanity
Millions have never tasted your philosophy.
How shameful that so few have ever imbibed
In what most learned men have found such rare delight;
Perhaps it is because they did not know
The value of your treatises—the merits of your lofty works.
You too have made a mark upon society;
Too few have recognized your worth—
Or utilized your rare sagacity,
But now that it has been revealed
We can expect your wisdom to bear fruit;
Far more than in the distant past—
Our heritage at last will be revived,
This nation growing richer, by
virture of your wisdom's gems.

NAME INDEX

SUBJECT INDEX

121